THE JOY OF
ABIDING

D1367478

JOHN GEORGE

publishers
SOLUTION
The Key to Publishing Possibilities

The Joy of Abiding
by John George

ISBN-13: 978-1-937925-23-9

Unless noted on scripture all quotes are from the New Revised Standard Version Bible (NRSV), copyright © 1989 the Division of Christian Education of the National Council of the Churches of Christ in the United States of America. Used by permission. All rights reserved.

English Standard Version (ESV)

When noted (ESV) The Holy Bible, English Standard Version. ESV® Text Edition: 2016. Copyright © 2001 by Crossway Bibles, a publishing ministry of Good News Publishers.

New King James Version (NKJV)

When noted (NKJV) scripture taken from the New King James Version®. Copyright © 1982 by Thomas Nelson. Used by permission. All rights reserved.

Holman Christian Standard Bible (HCSB)

When noted (HCSB) scripture is Copyright © 1999, 2000, 2002, 2003, 2009 by Holman Bible Publishers, Nashville Tennessee. All rights reserved.

New International Version (NIV)

The noted (NIV) Holy Bible, New International Version®, NIV® Copyright ©1973, 1978, 1984, 2011 by Biblica, Inc.® Used by permission. All rights reserved worldwide.

Cover & Interior Design: Megan Whitney Dillon
PublishersSolution.com

DEDICATION

Although there are many times in life to say, "Thank you," the following people are the ones I want to especially acknowledge and say "thank you for being my life-support team."

First, I thank my God for calling me, loving me, and allowing me to abide with Him. Second, my OAO (one and only) Judy for our sixty-four years. Third, our two children, Jeff and Jenna and their three children, respectively Levi, Micah, Noa and Kaitlin, Gabrielle, and Jonathan.

Beyond family, there are the many couples with whom we have been blessed to share both Sunday school and Bible Studies – around the corner, across the country and around the world. I am also thankful for the hundreds of students from high school through college, especially cadets at West Point, and students at Liberty University that I was privileged to both teach and mentor, applying the "iron sharpens iron" principle.

Finally, there has been one coach who has befriended me, encouraged me and patiently listened to "my" coaching tips – Liberty University Women's Basketball coach, Carey Green and his wife, Denise who have become "Special Friends."

I praise God for ALL with whom He has allowed me to cross paths, particularly spiritual paths, to help me grow.

CONTENT

INTRODUCTION

Over the past few months, I have been under Hospice care, a result of having terminal cancer. The chemotherapy has proven to be no longer useful in halting cancer's invasion of my body. So, a few months ago, the chemo was terminated, and the doctors told me that from then on, my new therapy would be to "make me comfortable" in my final days. Hence – Hospice.

I have never died before, so this caused me to give considerable consideration on how I would spend my last days. I had heard of those who went out "kicking, screaming, and swearing" and I didn't want that and prayed that wouldn't be the case.

I decided to share some indispensable thoughts with my beloved family, especially my grandchildren. A verse my grandchildren have heard me quote so many times is 3 John 1:4: *"I have no greater joy than to hear that my children are walking in the truth."* (ESV)

The key passage for this book is John 15:5-17. When looking at a passage, I sometimes like to waterski over it and enjoy the view. At other times, I want to skin dive into the passage for a complete understanding of its implications for my life. I have found that John 15:5-17 is one of those skin diving passages.

"Being a teacher for many years, I have learned how true the saying is, 'repetition is the mother of all learning.' In fact, this is perhaps the most intuitive principle of learning..."

The keyword for the passage is "abide." John 15:5 states *"I am the vine; you are the branches. Whoever abides in me and I in him, he it is that bears much fruit, for apart from me you can do nothing."* (ESV) This book has been gleaned from John 15:5-17. For now, I'll say that your life will count eternally for nothing if you do not thoroughly understand and lovingly apply "abiding" to your life.

As an introduction, I have briefly introduced the theme here. As we "skin dive" through the chapters, I will amplify my theme considerably. In Chapter One I have included a visual reminder of what it is to abide in Christ. As we dive even deeper into the remaining chapters, John 15:5-17 will become a beautiful picture of what the rest of your life could be.

Being a teacher for many years, I have learned how true the saying is, "repetition is the mother of all learning." In fact, this is perhaps the most intuitive principle of learning, which is traceable to ancient Egyptian and Chinese education, with records dating back approximately to 3000 B.C. In ancient Greece, Aristotle commented on the role of repetition in learning by saying "it is the frequent repetition that produces a natural tendency." But I think I like Zig Ziglar's quote about repetition the best, "Repetition is the mother of learning, the father of action, which makes it the architect of accomplishment."

So let me start laying the foundation of this book by quoting John 15:5-17:

> *"I am the vine; you are the branches. Those who abide in me and I in them bear much fruit because apart from me you can do nothing. Whoever does not abide in me is thrown away like a branch and withers; such branches are gathered, thrown into the fire, and burned. If you abide in me, and my words abide in you, ask for whatever you wish, and it will be done for you. My Father is glorified by this, that you bear much fruit and become my disciples. As the Father has loved me, so I have loved you; abide in my love. If you keep my commandments, you will abide in my love, just as I have kept my Father's commandments and abide in his love. **I have said these things to you so that my joy may be in you, and that your joy may be complete.***

This is my commandment, that you love one another as I have loved you. No one has greater love than this, to lay down one's life for one's friends. You are my friends if you do what I command you. I do not call you servants any longer, because the servant does not know what the master is doing; but I have called you friends because I have made known to you everything that I have heard from my Father. You did not choose me, but I chose you. And I appointed you to go and bear fruit, fruit that will last, so that the Father will give you whatever you ask him in my name. I am giving you these commands so that you may love one another."

It is critical that you fully understand the word "abide." Its definition is to accept or act by a rule, decision, or recommendation. For example "I said I would abide by their decision."

A much more common term today would be hanging out! In today's terms, I believe Christ meant spending all available time together in a loving relationship, thoroughly knowing those in the group in the hope these would be best friends, and everyone would comply with the rules and honor each other.

Of course, the group would form and stay together by God's grace alone, guided by His Word alone, be obedient to Him out of love alone, would follow His leading alone, and would love each other following His example alone.

As you "skin dive" through the following chapters, you will gain knowledge. We are told that "knowledge is power," but I have learned during my journey that knowledge is nothing unless that knowledge is applied! Your choice!

If you haven't picked up on the fact yet, this book is my departing love letter to all those I have loved through the years. I pray you will sense on every page that you were loved, accepted and appreciated every day of my life.

Dad, Grampy, Dr. George, John

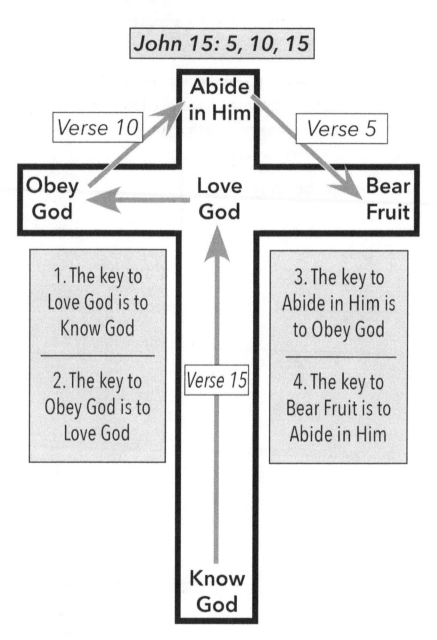

God's Formula of *"The Joy of Abiding"*

CHAPTER 1
The Three Greatest C's
The Building Blocks of Abiding

The 3 Greatest C's	
CALL	**PART 1**: JUSTIFICATION – OCCURS ONCE
	PART 2: SANTIFICATION – REST OF OUR LIFE
	PART 3: GLORIFICATION – IN HEAVEN
COMMANDMENT	**PART 1**: LOVING GOD WITH ALL OUR HEART
	PART 2: LOVING OUR NEIGHBOR
COMMISSION	MAKE DISCIPLES

"...but they who wait for the Lord shall renew their strength; they shall mount up with wings like eagles; they shall run and not be weary; they shall walk and not faint." Isaiah 40:31

The Greatest CALL – Part 1

Beyond writing this book as a love letter, I want all to know that there is a higher lifestyle than what the news media of all varieties would lead us to believe is the norm. I have called this alternative lifestyle *"The Joy of Abiding".* It's more commonly known name or label is "Christianity." That label is the result of a personal decision a person makes concerning salvation.

I have lived a long and blessed life and can attest to the truths and miracles of the New Testament, which have removed all doubts concerning Jesus' claim to being God.

So what is the Biblical means of becoming a Christian? According to the Bible, it is not the myriad of good works that we could do to impress God with our worthiness. To our great surprise, there is nothing we could do to earn our way into true Christianity and God's presence forever!

"For no human being will be justified in his sight by deeds prescribed by the law, for through the law comes the knowledge of sin." Romans 3:20

Our debt of sin is so great that we could never "pay" for it with good works. But God, in His infinite mercy and grace provided the only way for our salvation.

"All have sinned and fall short of the glory of God; they are now justified by his grace as a gift, through the redemption that is in Christ Jesus." Romans 3: 23-24

In His mercy, God sent His only Son, Jesus down to earth for 33 years to demonstrate living a sinless life and then take upon Himself our sins by means of a tragic death on a cross before God miraculously raised Him from the dead. So we have come now again to an introduction of the theme of this book, *"The Joy of Abiding!"*

Look at the promise in Matthew 11:28-30: *"Come to me, all you that are weary and are carrying heavy burdens, and I will give you rest. Take my yoke upon you, and learn from me; for I am gentle and humble in heart, and you will find rest for your souls. For my yoke is easy, and my burden is light."* This was God's response to

mankind's fatal position that we could not save ourselves. So, I repeat, God sent His beloved Son to live a sinless life thereby qualifying Him to take our sins upon Himself in order to bridge the gulf of sin to life with God.

For you who have already made the decision to follow Christ, I pray this book will supercharge you to new levels of Christian maturity. If you have already realized the truth taught in Romans 5:8: *"But God proves His love for us in that while we still were sinners Christ died for us,"* then you can believe John 8:36 and know you are "set free:" *"So if the Son makes you free, you will be free indeed."*

Then you can believe John 8:36 and know you are "set free." *"So if the Son makes you free, you will be free indeed."*

This first call to salvation, theologically referred to as justification, is the act of being freed from the penalty of sin, which is directed to all who are walking through life alone, and to those who are heavy laden or burdened by sin. They are carrying more than they are designed to carry. Justification is God's act of removing the guilt and penalty of sin while at the same time making a sinner righteous through Christ's atoning sacrifice.

An illustration that helped me grasp the essence of the term "heavy laden" is like when a ship is designed initially, it is given a watermark to designate the load that it may safely carry without fear of capsizing or sinking. Visualize the headline stories of refugees seeking to escape persecution who overloaded boats only to capsize and die in storms at sea. There were more than 2,500 deaths of people trying to cross the Mediterranean to Europe in 2017.

The "Five Solas"

Because of the widespread misunderstanding concerning what is necessary to become a Christian, I am compelled to present the "theology of justification" referred to as the Five Solas.

The Five Solas were first defined during the Reformation that occurred 500 years ago. These five doctrines preclude belief in any other person or religion. The Latin word *sola* means "alone" or "only" in English. The Five Solas define five fundamental beliefs of the Protestant Reformation. These are the five pillars, which the Reformers believed to be essentials of the Christian life and practice. Within these Five Solas comes a lifestyle that is known as Christianity. They are:

1. Sola Scriptura ("by Scripture alone")

2. Sola Fide ("by faith alone")

3. Sola Gratia ("by grace alone")

4. Solus Christus ("Christ alone")

5. Soli Deo Gloria ("glory to God alone")

Because each of these is critical to one's becoming a Christian, let me very briefly discuss what each means.

1. Sola Scriptura ("by Scripture Alone")

The Bible, the only inspired Word of God and the only source of Christian doctrine tells us in 2 Timothy 3:16-17:

"All scripture is inspired by God and is useful for teaching, for reproof, for correction, and for training in righteousness, so that everyone who belongs to God may be proficient, equipped for every good work."

The Bible gives us a lifelong means of directing our life when we use the question, "What does the Scripture teach about a matter?" That must always be our rule of thought and action.

2. Sola Fide ("By Faith Alone")

We are justified and accepted by God by faith alone, apart from works of the law, apart from sacraments, apart from anything else except the other solas. If we believe that the Scriptures exclude works in any form as a means of our salvation, then logically we are saved by faith alone. The Bible is clear. We are saved through faith alone, and through nothing that we do.

Justification (freed from the PENALTY of sin) comes through faith in Christ alone. There are NO OTHER MEANS. If we believe that we have any part in our justification, then we are saying that we had to help the atoning work of Christ and that His death was not a sufficient price.

3. Sola Gratia ("By Grace Alone")

Sola Gratia is the teaching that salvation comes by God's grace. It is simply "unmerited favor" only — NOT something deserved by the sinner. It is an unearned gift from God.

Ephesians 2:8-9 states, *"For by grace you have been saved through faith, and this is not your own doing; it is the gift of God— not the result of works, so that no one may boast."*

4. Solus Christus ("By Christ Alone")

Solus Christus emphasizes that salvation can only be found through the death and resurrection of Christ alone. Scripture leaves no wiggle room on this point.

John 14:6: *"Jesus said to him, I am the way, and the truth, and the life. No one comes to the Father except through me."*

Christ did not say that He is a way, a truth or a life. He clearly stated that no man comes to the Father except through Him. God's Word leaves no room for any idea that there can be salvation apart from Christ.

If salvation could be found through Muhammad, Buddha, Krishna or good works, then there would be no reason for Jesus to die. But Christ was the only person who could satisfy God's wrath due to our sinfulness, and therefore atone for our sins because of His sinlessness. He took upon Himself our sins and justified those who repent and put their trust in Him alone.

Our acceptance by God is not based upon any righteousness produced by ourselves. Instead, it is based on the righteous life and atoning death of Christ alone. Galatians 2:16, *"...yet we know that a person is justified not by the works of the law but through faith in Jesus Christ. And we have come to believe in Christ Jesus, so that we might be justified by faith in Christ, and not by doing the works of the law, because no one will be justified by the works of the law."*

5. Soli Deo Gloria – ("Glory to God Alone")

Belief in God alone removes all grounds for boasting and for claiming merit before God. It gives all glory for the salvation of the sinner to God alone — the Father, Son and Holy Spirit. Salvation is by grace alone through faith alone in Christ alone, as revealed in His Word alone, and for His glory alone. Through faith, His righteousness is applied to us. All we can bring to Him for salvation are our sins. We can supply nothing!

1 Corinthians 1:30-31: *"He is the source of your life in Christ Jesus, who became for us wisdom from God, and righteousness and sanctification and redemption, so that, as it is written, Let the one who boasts, boast in the Lord."*

Romans 11:36 summarizes it all, *"For from him and through him and to him are all things. To him be the glory forever. Amen."*

Everything we do should be for His glory, and everything God does or allows to happen is for His glory. We can never fully understand why God allows certain things to happen, but as believers, we can rest assured that the sovereign God of the universe, the One who knows all things, knows best. Those things will bring glory to God alone – *Soli Deo Gloria.* Let us learn from this and give God ALL the glory because He and He alone is worthy.

A significant *"The Joy of Abiding"* blessing that came to me has been the knowledge that no circumstance will ever come upon me that God will not be available when I call. This truth provides peace and rest for my soul that is available nowhere else on earth. Insurance can't provide it; wealth can't, nothing can!

This truth became very real to me when I heard the words that I had Stage 4 cancer. After two years of fighting cancer, I was told that the only chemo beneficial for my type of cancer was no longer effective. My chemo was terminated, and efforts were planned to make me as comfortable as possible. Let me tell you that from the bottom of my heart that God's love, presence, and promise for a future have been sufficient to sustain me.

The Greatest CALL – Part 2

A point that I can't repeat enough because I have found that many Christians don't fully understand it is that God's call has three parts: (1) Justification, freedom from the penalty of sin, which is instantaneous and occurs once in a lifetime; (2) Sanctification, freedom from the power of sin, which happens moment by moment throughout one's lifetime as a Christian; and (3) Glorification, freedom from the presence of sin which occurs at our physical death or the Rapture (the return of Christ for the Church) whichever comes first. Justification is exclusively a work of God through the Holy Spirit. Sanctification means we work with the Holy Spirit to "work out our salvation," i.e. become more Christlike in what we think, say and do, such as becoming more loving, forgiving, etc.

So a Christian's CALL will change from justification, which is freedom from the penalty of sin, to sanctification, freedom from the power of sin. We come to God as sinners. Upon acceptance of Christ as our Savior, we are declared from that point to be saints.

Regretfully, saints still sin, and so comes the need for lifelong sanctification. So, you can say, God's CALL to come to Him endures throughout our entire lives. To repeat, justification freed us from the penalty of sin; sanctification frees us from the power of sin. Justification is instantaneous. Sanctification is a lifetime process.

So you can say, God's CALL to come to Him endures throughout our entire lives. It is new every morning and with us all day every day as explained in Lamentations 3:22-24:

> *The steadfast love of the Lord never ceases,*
>   *his mercies never come to an end;*
> *they are new every morning;*
>   *great is your faithfulness.*
> *"The Lord is my portion," says my soul,*
>   *"therefore I will hope in him."*

Focusing now on the second part of the greatest CALL, sanctification, we see how Scripture illustrates the necessity of abiding in Christ.

John 15:5: *"I am the vine, you are the branches. Those who abide in me and I in them bear much fruit because apart from me you can do nothing."*

John 15:10: *"If you keep my commandments, you will abide in my love, just as I have kept my Father's commandments and abide in his love."*

John 15:15: *"I do not call you slaves any longer, because the slave does not know what the master is doing; but I have called you friends because I have made known to you everything that I have heard from my Father."*

The key word from this passage is "abide." Again, let me skin dive to hopefully give a fuller understanding of this word. Some dictionary insights follow:

a. to act in accord with

b. to submit to; agree to; *to abide by the court's decision*

c. to remain steadfast or faithful to; keep*: if you make a promise, abide by it*

So, in the context of John 15:10, abiding would be ensuring one's actions remained faithful to and were in accord with and submitted to God's will. Hence, we can now see that obedience is the personal requirement for abiding.

God's CALL to Sanctification

Remember justification is instantaneous and occurs only once in one's lifetime, sanctification occurs moment by moment throughout one's lifetime as a Christian. Glorification occurs upon one's death or at the Rapture. Justification is exclusively a work of God through the Holy Spirit. In sanctification, we work with the Holy Spirit to *"work out"* our salvation in becoming more Christ-like in character.

I must repeat the point that we come to God as sinners. Upon acceptance of Christ as our Savior, we are declared henceforth to be saints. We all know that saints still sin, and so comes the need for sanctification. As I stated previously, justification freed us from the penalty of sin, sanctification frees us from the power of sin. Again, this means justification is instantaneous, and sanctification is a lifetime process. Hence, God's CALL to come to Him endures throughout our entire lives. The blessings of *"The Joy of Abiding"* begins with God's CALL to everlasting life.

The Greatest COMMANDMENT - Part 1

"Teacher, which commandment in the law is the greatest?' He said to him, 'You shall love the Lord your God with all your heart, and with all your soul, and with all your mind.' This is the greatest and first commandment. And a second is like it: 'You shall love your neighbor as yourself.' On these two commandments hang all the law and the prophets." Matthew 22:36-40

As you can see, this quotation contains two commands, a great one, and a second one. First, let's discuss the great one: *"'You shall love the Lord your God with all your heart, and with all your soul, and with all your mind.'"* In the Greatest Call – Part 1, it was all about God's acting on our behalf. Now in the Greatest Commandment, it appears to be all about our responsibility to first love God and then to love our neighbor as our self. As we will discover in Chapter 2, the Holy Spirit will be very active in working out the greatest COMMANDMENT.

To be able to obey this commandment, we must first understand what it means to love God. Surprisingly, it does not mean what most people would think it does, a warm feeling. There are numerous words today that have lost their meaning by overuse. Two of them are "cool" and "love." When everything is cool, nothing is; and so with love. I love that puppy; I love that shirt, I love that song, I love that book, and on and on.... God's

Word provides a definition of love that is radically different from our definition. We see that in John 14:21. *"They who have my commandments and keep them are those who love me, and those who love me will be loved by my Father, and I will love them and reveal myself to them."*

Here we see that love from God's perspective is not measured primarily by warm fuzzy feelings, but by obedience to His commandments, or as we have just learned, by abiding by them. His criteria states that our love is to be measured by *"...all your heart and with all your soul and with all your mind."* As I've just written, the *"all your heart"* refers not simply to feelings for God, but loyalty to His commandments. *"All your soul"* and *"all your mind"* are merely emphasizing that such love is measured by its completeness. Most important: one's abiding is directly in proportion to one's obedience.

Going back to our theme, *"The Joy of Abiding,"* we have seen that it begins with God's offering freedom from the penalty of sin made possible by the sacrifice of His Son Jesus on our behalf. This offer required us to acknowledge and confess our sin and accept Christ's offering by faith. This was a once and for all offering that was followed by a continuing 24/7 offering from God never to leave us or forsake us. Thus, His commitment was total and unending.

Now considering the second greatest "C," the Greatest Commandment, we see the nature of our commitment to God—that it is also to be 24/7!

The Greatest COMMANDMENT - Part 2

The initial greatest C, the Call, has three parts, and the second greatest C, Commandment has two. We are not only commanded to love God totally, but we are commanded to "love your neighbor as yourself." I find the second command to be more difficult than the first. I find it more difficult to love the imperfect neighbor unequivocally than a perfect God. This second part of the second commandment is often referred to as "The Golden Rule," *"Do unto others as you would have them do unto you."* This provides a simple way to judge your behavior. Would you want someone to treat you that way, say that to you, etc.? And it goes deeper than that. It includes, not only what you would not like done to you by others, but perhaps the more difficult, what you would like done to you or for you. Think for a moment how *"The Joy of Abiding"* would be if people committed themselves to this second commandment!

The Greatest COMMISSION - Part 3

We come now to the third greatest C, the COMMISSION. This passage states Jesus' words that God had given Him all authority *"in heaven and on earth."* And exercising this authority, He was commissioning His disciples to go to all nations to make disciples. To apply this verse today, we must update changes that have occurred. First, Jesus died and returned to heaven as presented in Acts 1:1-9:

> *"In the first book, Theophilus, I wrote about all that Jesus did and taught from the beginning until the day when he was taken up to heaven, after giving instructions through*

the Holy Spirit to the apostles whom he had chosen. After his suffering he presented himself alive to them by many convincing proofs, appearing to them during forty days and speaking about the kingdom of God. While staying with them, he ordered them not to leave Jerusalem, but to wait there for the promise of the Father. "This," he said, "is what you have heard from me; for John baptized with water, but you will be baptized with the Holy Spirit not many days from now.

"So when they had come together, they asked him, "Lord, is this the time when you will restore the kingdom to Israel?" He replied, "It is not for you to know the times or periods that the Father has set by his authority. But you will receive power when the Holy Spirit has come upon you; and you will be my witnesses in Jerusalem, in all Judea and Samaria, and to the ends of the earth." When he had said this, as they were watching, he was lifted up, and a cloud took him out of their sight."

These verses have had a special meaning for me all these 60 years. On June 4, 1958, I graduated from the United States Military Academy at West Point. Two other very significant events occurred that day. That morning, I was commissioned as a Second Lieutenant of Infantry in the United States Army. Along with all my graduating classmates, I took the following oath that morning:

"I, John David George, Jr., having been appointed an officer in the Army of the United States, in the grade of Second Lieutenant, do solemnly swear that I will support and defend the Constitution of the United

States against all enemies, foreign and domestic, that I will bear true faith and allegiance to the same; that I take this obligation freely, without any mental reservations or purpose of evasion; and that I will well and faithfully discharge the duties of the office upon which I am about to enter; So help me God."

Three hours later, I took another oath before God that read as follows:

"I, John David George, Jr., take thee, Judith Elaine Early, to be my wedded wife, to have and to hold from this day forward, for better for worse, for richer for poorer, in sickness and in health, to love and to cherish, till death us do part, according to God's holy ordinance; and thereto I plight thee my troth."

Then, I placed the ring on Judy's finger with the following words:

"With this ring, I thee wed, with my body I thee worship, and with all my worldly goods I thee endow: In the name of the Father, and of the Son, and of the Holy Ghost. Amen."

Then three years later while serving on Okinawa in June of 1961, I knelt by my bed, confessing twenty-five years of sins and committing my life from then on to God in Christ.

The third greatest C, the COMMISSION is a command left by Jesus for every follower of His, found in Matthew 28:16-20:

"Now the eleven disciples went to Galilee, to the mountain to which Jesus had directed them. When they saw him, they worshiped him; but some doubted. And Jesus came and said to them, "All authority in heaven and on earth has been given to me. Go therefore and make disciples of all nations, baptizing them in the name of the Father and of the Son and of the Holy Spirit, and teaching them to obey everything that I have commanded you. And remember, I am with you always, to the end of the age."

My presentation of the third greatest C, COMMISSION has been introductory because the remainder of this book describes how the Holy Spirit makes disciples of us and how we join with the Spirit in bringing others to Christ.

In Chapter 8 we will talk about how every believer has their own story, or personal testimony of what God has done in their lives. Keep in mind; we do not make disciples, the Holy Spirit does, but He has chosen us to co-labor with Him. He does this by way of the "fruit of the Spirit" which we manifest to others as we are transformed by our love for God. As we will discover in Chapter 3, there are nine dimensions of this singular fruit: love, joy, peace, patience, kindness, goodness, faithfulness, gentleness, and self-control. It is time we move forward in our quest to discover *"The Joy of Abiding."*

the **Fruit** of the **Spirit**

is *love* JOY

peace patience

KINDNESS

GOODNESS

faithfulness

GENTLENESS

& self-control

Galatians 5: 22-23

CHAPTER 2
The Holy Spirit's and Your Ministries

In Chapter 1, I presented you with what I called the Three Greatest "C's." What God was doing in those three "C's" was the most significant paradigm shift in the history of mankind. God had created the world and mankind. It was a perfect world where sinless mankind lived in a perfect garden until Adam and Eve sinned by disobeying God. Out of love for mankind, God sent His Son, Jesus to live a sinless life to qualify Him to die for mankind's sin. The Old Testament relates the first paradigm, God's eventual choosing of Abraham and the nation Israel to be His chosen people. Eventually, that relationship became shattered by Israel's continued disobedience, so God established a new paradigm to reconcile man's sinfulness. The four Gospels relate the paradigm shift from salvation by keeping the Law to salvation through Christ's death and resurrection.

God the Father was the dominant initiator in the Old Testament (See Romans 11), Christ the dominant initiator in the Gospels, and the Holy Spirit for the remainder of the New Testament and the 2000+ years since then.

Thus, the Holy Spirit is now the dominant initiator of God's will to seek to conform mankind to the character of Christ. Review the Overview of the Christian Life diagram below:

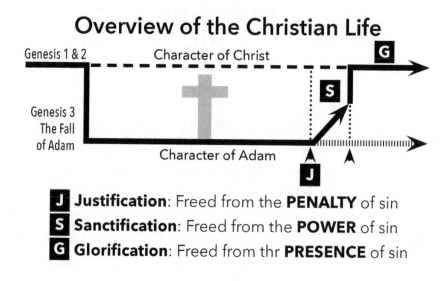

Overview of the Christian Life

Genesis 1 & 2   Character of Christ

Genesis 3
The Fall
of Adam   Character of Adam

J **Justification**: Freed from the **PENALTY** of sin
S **Sanctification**: Freed from the **POWER** of sin
G **Glorification**: Freed from thr **PRESENCE** of sin

We begin with the assumption that at some point in the past (left triangle "J"), you accepted Christ as your Lord and Savior. You are now somewhere in time before the second triangle, which represents the Second Coming of Christ (Rapture) at which time you will be raised up to heaven, and your character will be completed.

Now we return to the second part of the Greatest COMMAND for the Holy Spirit's challenge in helping mankind achieve the Character of Christ: *"Teacher, which is the great commandment in the Law?" And he said to him, "You shall love the Lord your God with all your heart and with all your soul and with all your mind. "This is the great and first commandment. And a second is like it: You shall love your neighbor as yourself. On these two commandments depend all the Law and the Prophets."* Matthew 22:36-40 (ESV)

In Chapter 1, we considered Part 1 of the Greatest Commandment summarized by the concept of "abiding" with God. Now we turn to the second part, *"you shall love your neighbor as yourself."* Matthew 12 provides a warning starting in verse 33-37: *"Either make the tree good and its fruit good, or make the tree bad and its fruit bad, for the tree is known by its fruit. You brood of vipers! How can you speak good, when you are evil? For out of the abundance of the heart the mouth speaks. The good person out of his good treasure brings forth good, and the evil person out of his evil treasure brings forth evil. I tell you, on the day of judgment people will give account for every careless word they speak. For by your words you will be justified, and by your words, you will be condemned."* (ESV)

The question I have heard over the past 57 years is,"Do I have the ability to carry out the second part of the Greatest Commandment?" The resounding answer to that question is, "Yes!" I can say that because of the answer to another frequently asked question which is, "Where does the Holy Spirit reside today?"

Once again, let's skin dive into where the Holy Spirit resides and its implications concerning our theme of abiding. The Scriptures are clear. The answer is found in all translations of Scripture, specifically 1 Corinthians 3:16 – *"Do you not know that you are God's temple and that God's Spirit dwells in you?"* He's where? He resides in believers!

Now join me again for some of the most joyous skin diving there could be. If I were to give it a new name today, I would call it "hanging out." It would be analogous to having a best friend move into our home and hearts, wanting to "hang out" with us in every area of our lives.

> "Here we learn the Holy Spirit is not far away like some distant star, **but He is in you** and now, abiding takes on a whole new perspective. If I were to give it a new name today, I would call it 'hanging out.'"

But the skin diving doesn't end there. When I thought about this revelation, I realized I'd need to clean house for my special friend from heaven. The first room I'd want to clean would be my heart. I used to think it was the room named "my will," but again Scriptures are sure. *"Above all else, guard your heart, for everything you do flows from it,"* Proverbs 3:5-6. Other rooms include the will, the soul, the mind, the body, garage, basement, etc.

From these verses, we can see that one of the Holy Spirit's major missions in these days is to change mankind's heart and resulting vocabulary to reflect that of loving one another. So let's begin with John 13:34-35: *"A new commandment I give to you, that you love one another: just as I have loved you, you also are to love one another. By this, all people will know that you are my disciples, if you have love for one another."* Through the years, I have been surprised by how few Christians realize there are at least 29 "One Another's" in Scripture. To me, LOVE ONE ANOTHER may be portrayed as a diamond. And what gives a diamond its beauty? In this case, the 28 facets that add depth and breadth to our heart's understanding of *"Love One Another"*. The following chart depicts the 28 other "One Another's." I should point out that the four subtitles are the way I grouped them, not the Holy Spirit.

HOW TO
LOVE ONE ANOTHER
28 Scriptural Ways to Strengthen
Sanctify, Share, and Stimulate Your Love For Each Other
John 13:34-35

To Strengthen Love ————————————
1. **Be members** of each other – Romans 12:5
2. **Accept** each other – Romans 17:7
3. **Be devoted** to each other – Romans 12:10
4. **Confess your faults** to each other – James 5:16
5. **Edify** each other – Romans 14:19
6. **Live in harmony** with each other – Romans 12:16
7. **Fellowship** with each other – I John 1:7

To Sanctify Love ————————————
1. **Honor** each other I Peter 4:9
2. **Forgive** each other – Ephesians 4:32
3. **Be tender-hearted** with each other – Ephesians 4:32
4. **Submit** to each other – Ephesians 4:21
5. **Admonish** each other – Romans 15:14
6. **Forbear** each other – Ephesians 4:1-6, 32
7. **Be kind** to each other – Ephesians 4:32

To Share Love ————————————
1. **Serve** each other – Galatians 5:13
2. **Bear** each other's burdens – Galatains 6:2
3. **Comfort** each other – I Thessalonians 4:18
4. *Greet* each other – I Corinthians 16:20
5. **Teach** each other – Colossians 3:16
6. **Have peace** with each other – Mark 9:50
7. **Be hospitable** to each other – Romans 12:10

To Stimulate Love ————————————
1. **Serve** each other – I Peter 4:10
2. **Care** for each other – I Corinthians 12:25
3. **Have compassion** for each other – I Peter 3:8
4. **Esteem** each other – Philemon 2:3
5. **Exhort** each other – Hebrews 3:13; 10:24-25
6. **Pray** for each other – James 5:16
7. **Stir-up** each other – Hebrews 10:24

Moving on to the Goal of the Christian Life - MATURITY

(Ephesians 4:11-16)

- Love God with all your heart, mind, soul, and strength (Matthew 22:37-40)

- Consistently evidence the Fruit of the Spirit in all areas of your life: Love, Joy, Peace, Patience, Kindness, Goodness, Faithfulness, Gentleness, and Self-Control (Galatians 5:22-24)

- Know and apply the 29 "One Another's" in all of your Christian relationships

- Develop in your maturity from dependence to independence (physical, financial, and emotional) and be developed interdependently with others

Another complementary ministry of the Holy Spirit is entitled the "Fruit of the Spirit." As noted in the following listing there, these are nine qualities, which appear to operate in threes as listed below (See Galatians 5:22-23).

- **First three:** Habits of the mind that find their source in God

     love *(agape)* – unconquerable benevolence (1 Corinthians 13:4-7)

     joy *(chara)* – deep and abiding inner rejoicing in Christ

peace *(eirene)* – the tranquility that abides when one has absolute confidence that God is in control in every situation and circumstance

- **Second three:** Fortified by the first three would entail reaching out to others

    patience *(makrothumia)* – forbearance under provocation with no thought of retaliation

    kindness *(chrestotes)* – benevolence in action; it can only help

    goodness *(agathosune)* – most comprehensive form of goodness; includes rebuke and discipline when needed

- **Third three:** These final three guide the general conduct of a believer who is led by the Spirit

    faithfulness *(pistis)* – absolute integrity, trustworthiness, and reliability

    gentleness *(praetes)* – submissive to God's will, teachable, and considerate

    self-control *(egkrateia)* – use of an athlete's mastery of his body and the Christian's mastery of sex – physically fit and morally right

"Against such things, there is no law. Those who belong to Christ Jesus have crucified the sinful nature with its passions and desires." Galatians 5:23b-24

There is some confusion concerning the Fruit of the Spirit and the Gifts of the Spirit. Every believer may have all nine of the fruit. Concerning the Gifts of the Spirit, every believer has at least one of the gifts, but no one has them all (Note: the Spiritual Gifts will be identified and explained below). The Holy Spirit disperses these at the moment of conversion. These can be very influential in the Holy Spirit's ministries.

Second, the authority of the Old Testament was God the Father. In the New Testament, the authority through the Gospels was the second Person of the Trinity, Christ. Then, as presented in the passage above, that authority became the third Person of the Trinity, the Holy Spirit. The mission of the Holy Spirit is spelled out in Jesus' words in John 14:26 – *"But the Advocate, the Holy Spirit, whom the Father will send in my name, will teach you everything, and remind you of all that I have said to you."*

> "There is some confusion concerning the Fruit of the Spirit and the Gifts of the Spirit. Concerning the Gifts of the Spirit, every believer may have all nine of the fruit. Every believer has at least one of the gifts, but no one has them all."

Christ gave this commission to the original disciples. Today, Christ's disciples are those individuals who have heard and responded to His CALL to come unto Him and His COMMANDMENT to love Him and one another. He now, through the power of the Holy Spirit, COMMISSIONS us, His disciples, to go into all nations to make other disciples.

It should be re-emphasized at this point that we are not the ones who make believers. It is solely a work of God, the Holy Spirit, who has been chosen to co-labor with Him in bearing His fruit and making disciples of believers. Galatians 5:22-24 outlines His fruit and a prerequisite for our part in it.

"By contrast, the fruit of the Spirit is love, joy, peace, patience, kindness, generosity, faithfulness, gentleness, and self-control. There is no law against such things. And those who belong to Christ Jesus have crucified the flesh with its passions and desires."

The Apostle Paul is saying that the former Paul was not the same person. In his coming to Christ, he had taken all of his previous sinful self to the cross to be crucified there with Christ, which is the prerequisite of his becoming a disciple of Christ and our prerequisite, too.

Perhaps the most powerful and significant ministry of the Holy Spirit is the parceling out of spiritual gifts which occurs when one accepts Christ as their Savior. The gifts are for the most part taken from Romans 12, 1 Corinthians 12, and Ephesians 4. A Christian may possess more than one of these gifts, but no one has them all.

SPIRITUAL GIFTS				
Gift	Romans 12	Corinthians 12	Ephesians 4	Other
Special Gifts - EQUIP God's people				
Prophecy	X	X	X	
Evangelists			X	
Pastors			X	
Teachers	X		X	
Missionary				X
Martyrdom				X
Voluntary poverty				X
Speaking Gifts - EXPLAIN God's truth				
Exhortation	X			
Prophesying		X	X	
Teaching		X		
Message of Wisdom			X	
Knowledge		X		
Serving Gifts - ENABLE God's work				
Administration		X		
Discernment		X		
Faith		X		
Giving	X			
Helps			X	
Hospitality				X
Leadership	X			
Serving	X			
Showing Mercy	X			
Sign Gifts - ESTABLISH God's authority				
Healing		X		
Interpretation of Tongues			X	
Miracles		X		
Tongues		X		

Spiritual Gifts
1 Corinthians 12:1-31

"Now concerning spiritual gifts, brothers and sisters, I do not want you to be uninformed. You know that when you were pagans, you were enticed and led astray to idols that could not speak. Therefore I want you to understand that no one speaking by the Spirit of God ever says "Let Jesus be cursed!" and no one can say "Jesus is Lord" except by the Holy Spirit.

"Now there are varieties of gifts, but the same Spirit; and there are varieties of services, but the same Lord; and there are varieties of activities, but it is the same God who activates all of them in everyone.

"To each is given the manifestation of the Spirit for the common good. To one is given through the Spirit the utterance of wisdom, and to another the utterance of knowledge according to the same Spirit, to another faith by the same Spirit, to another gifts of healing by the one Spirit, to another the working of miracles, to another prophecy, to another the discernment of spirits, to another various kinds of tongues, to another the interpretation of tongues. All these are activated by one and the same Spirit, who allots to each one individually just as the Spirit chooses."

One Body with Many Members

"For just as the body is one and has many members, and all the members of the body, though many, are one body, so it is with Christ. For in the one Spirit we were all baptized into one body—Jews or Greeks, slaves or free—and we were all made to drink of one Spirit.

"Indeed, the body does not consist of one member but of many. If the foot would say, "Because I am not a hand, I do not belong to the body," that would not make it any less a part of the body. And if the ear would say, "Because I am not an eye, I do not belong to the body," that would not make it any less a part of the body. If the whole body were an eye, where would the hearing be? If the whole body were hearing, where would the sense of smell be? But as it is, God arranged the members in the body, each one of them, as he chose. If all were a single member, where would the body be? As it is, there are many members, yet one body.

"The eye cannot say to the hand, "I have no need of you," nor again the head to the feet, "I have no need of you." On the contrary, the members of the body that seem to be weaker are indispensable, and those members of the body that we think less honorable we clothe with greater honor, and our less respectable members are treated with greater respect; whereas our more respectable members do not need this. But God has so arranged the body, giving the greater honor to the inferior member, that there may be no dissension within the body, but the members may have the same care for one another. If one member suffers,

all suffer together with it; if one member is honored, all rejoice together with it.

"Now you are the body of Christ and individually members of it. And God has appointed in the church first apostles, second prophets, third teachers; then deeds of power, then gifts of healing, forms of assistance, forms of leadership, various kinds of tongues. Are all apostles? Are all prophets? Are all teachers? Do all work miracles? Do all possess gifts of healing? Do all speak in tongues? Do all interpret? But strive for the greater gifts. And I will show you a still more excellent way."

Romans 12:1-8

"I appeal to you, therefore, brothers and sisters, by the mercies of God, to present your bodies as a living sacrifice, holy and acceptable to God, which is your spiritual worship. Do not be conformed to this world, but be transformed by the renewing of your minds, so that you may discern what is the will of God—what is good and acceptable and perfect.

"For by the grace given to me, I say to everyone among you not to think of yourself more highly than you ought to think, but to think with sober judgment, each according to the measure of faith that God has assigned. For as in one body we have many members, and not all the members have the same function, so we, who are many, are one body in Christ, and individually we are members one of another. We have gifts that differ according to the grace

given to us: prophecy, in proportion to faith; ministry, in ministering; the teacher, in teaching; the exhorter, in exhortation; the giver, in generosity; the leader, in diligence; the compassionate, in cheerfulness."

Ephesians 4:11-13

"The gifts he gave were that some would be apostles, some prophets, some evangelists, some pastors and teachers, to equip the saints for the work of ministry, for building up the body of Christ, until all of us come to the unity of the faith and of the knowledge of the Son of God, to maturity, to the measure of the full stature of Christ."

Definitions of Spiritual Gifts Specifically Listed in the Bible:

ADMINISTRATION: 1 Corinthians 12:28 – to steer the body toward the accomplishment of God-given goals and directives by planning, organizing, and supervising others (Greek Word: *kubernesis* - to steer, guide, helmsmen)

APOSTLE: Ephesians 4:11; 1 Corinthians 12:28 – to be sent forth to new frontiers with the Gospel, providing leadership over church bodies and maintaining authority over spiritual matters pertaining to the church (Greek Word: *apostolos* – *apo*: from; *stello*: send – one sent forth)

DISCERNMENT: 1 Corinthians 12:10 – to clearly distinguish truth from error by judging whether the behavior or teaching is from God, Satan, human error, or human power

EVANGELISM: Ephesians 4:11 – to be a messenger of the Good News of the Gospel (Greek Word: *euaggelistes* – preacher of Gospel; *eu*: well, *angelos*: message – messenger of good)

EXHORTATION: Romans 12:8 – to come alongside someone with words of encouragement, comfort, consolation, and counsel to help them be all God wants them to be (Greek Word: *paraklesis* – calling to one's side)

FAITH: 1 Corinthians 12:8-10 – to be firmly persuaded of God's power and promises to accomplish His will and purpose and to display such a confidence in Him and His Word that circumstances and obstacles do not shake that conviction

GIVING: Romans 12:8 – to share what material resources you have with liberality and cheerfulness without thought of return

HELPS: 1 Corinthians 12:28 – to render support or assistance to others in the body to free them up for ministry

HOSPITALITY: 1 Peter 4:9,10 – to warmly welcome people, even strangers, into one's home or church as a means of serving those in need of food or lodging (Greek Word: *philoxenos* – love of strangers; *philos* – love; *xenos* – stranger)

KNOWLEDGE: 1 Corinthians 12:8 – to seek to learn as much about the Bible as possible through the gathering of much information and the analyzing of that data

MARTYRDOM: 1 Corinthians 13:3 – to give over one's life to suffer for/or to be put to death for the cause of Christ

MERCY: Romans 12:8 – to be sensitive toward those who are suffering, whether physically, mentally, or emotionally, to feel genuine sympathy with their misery, speaking words of compassion but more so caring for them with deeds of love to help alleviate their distress

MIRACLES: 1 Corinthians 12:10,28 – to be enabled by God to perform mighty acts that witnesses acknowledge to be of supernatural origin and means

MISSIONARY: Ephesians 3:6-8 – to be able to minister in another culture

PASTOR: Ephesians 4:11 – to be responsible for spiritually caring for, protecting, guiding, and feeding a group of believers entrusted to one's care

PROPHECY: Romans 12:6; 1 Corinthians 12:10; Ephesians 4:11 – to speak forth the message of God to His people (Greek Word: *prophetes* - the forth-telling of the will of God; 'pro'-*forth*; '*phemi*'- to speak)

SERVICE: Romans 12:7 – to identify undone tasks in God's work, however menial, and use available resources to get the job done (Greek Word: *diakonia* – deacon, attendant *'diako'* – to run errands)

TEACHING: Romans 12:7; 1 Corinthians 1 2:28; Ephesians 4: 11 – to instruct others in the Bible in a logical, systematic way to communicate pertinent information for true understanding and growth

INTERPRETATION OF TONGUES: 1 Corinthians 12:10; 14:27,28 – to translate the message of someone who has spoken in tongues

VOLUNTARY POVERTY: 1 Corinthians 13:3 – to purposely live an impoverished lifestyle to serve and aid others with your material resources

WISDOM: 1 Corinthians 12:8 – to apply knowledge to life in such a way as to make spiritual truths quite relevant and practical in proper decision-making and daily life situations

Bottom Line: The Holy Spirit has given you at least one spiritual gift to increase your effectiveness in ministry. Identify and thoroughly study this area of ministry, determine to know and apply your gift(s) today.

It's time now to bring Chapter 2 to a conclusion. Specifically, we need to make the application. Whereas God and Christ were the main characters in Chapter 1, the Holy Spirit and you became the focus of Chapter 2.

Theologically, Chapter 2 dealt mainly with the second part of the second Greatest "C," to love your neighbor as yourself. I began with presentations of the scriptural 29 "One Another's" that add breadth and depth to chart headline – "Love One Another." I suggest you study each of these carefully and make every effort to practice them and to integrate them into your daily walk with the Lord and the "One Another's" in your world. In a similar ministry, the Holy Spirit manages nine spiritual fruit. For their maximum effectiveness, these are most often applied in groups of three as demonstrated in the listing in this chapter accompanying my presentation of the fruit.

Since we share this ministry with the Holy Spirit, its success depends on you and me. Each one of us has one or more of the gifts. I recommend that each of you discover your spiritual gift(s). Different ministries have formed tests for identifying one's spiritual gift(s). Many resources are located on the Internet at SpiritualGiftsTesting.com. The one I found particularly helpful was the Ministry Tools Resource Center.

CHAPTER 3
Prayer

P rayer is the most important ministry that mankind has! I'm not talking about our morning quiet time, but as a moment-by-moment, minute-by-minute, 24/7 relationship with our God! That means, "hanging out" all day every day with the Holy Spirit as "Best friends."

In Chapter 1, recall the 3 Greatest "Cs." They meant coming to Him when He CALLS, LOVING Him "with all your heart and with all your soul and with all your mind," and ministering for Him. The truth is that making disciples is a direct command for all Christians and that loving Him means obeying Him. Collectively – when these prerequisites are combined, we have an abiding relationship!

When Should We Pray?

We should be in a constant attitude of prayer. Life gets busy and once we are awake and up for the day, it is vital that we don't forget to be grateful to God for a new day. Make it a habit of getting up with a prayer or praying while getting ready for a new day – even while in the shower. There is never a wrong time to pray, and the best part is that God is never too busy to hear us! *"The steadfast love of the Lord never ceases; his mercies never come to an end. They are new every morning. Great is your faithfulness."* Lamentations 3:22-23

Beginning each day with gratitude and praising God for another day will also help make a habit of bringing many we love to mind, lifting up a prayer for each one. There may be significant things throughout the day that need prayer – a business meeting, an upcoming birth or wedding, or a sick friend who needs prayer. If we start the day thinking of others before ourselves, we will be blessed, and it will help our day start out on a positive note having had our first conversation of the day with God.

Matthew 6:9–15

"Pray then in this way: Our Father in heaven, hallowed be your name. Your kingdom come. Your will be done, on earth as it is in heaven. Give us this day our daily bread. And forgive us our debts, as we also have forgiven our debtors. And do not bring us to the time of trial, but rescue us from the evil one.

"For if you forgive others their trespasses, your heavenly Father will also forgive you; but if you do not forgive others, neither will your Father forgive your trespasses."

So as we dig into the practice of prayer let us look at a few acrostics that have made my prayer life stronger, more effective and meaningful.

The Meaning of A-C-T-S when it comes to Prayer		
Acrostic: ACTS		
A	**Adoration**	Adoration is worship, honor, reverence, exalting and esteeming God for who He is
C	**Confession***	1 John 1:9 states, *"If we confess our sins, he who is faithful and just will forgive us our sins and cleanse us from all unrighteousness"*
T	**Thanksgiving**	Everything you have is from God; thank Him continually for His goodness
S	**Supplication**	Supplication means "to plead humbly." While thought of as a prayer, it can be used in any situation which you must ask someone in power for help or a favor

CONFESSION*		
Acrostic: GRIEF		
G	**Genuine**	I will feel genuine heartache over my sin
R	**Repent**	I will repent of my sin
I	**Immediately**	I will correct it immediately
E	**Expect**	I will expect forgiveness but realize the cost of that forgiveness
F	**Faithful**	I will return to being faithful to my Lord, better not bitter

Adoration - A

What is Adoration?

Adoration is worship, honor, reverence, exalting and esteeming God for who He is.

Applying the ACTS formula for prayer, we begin with the A for adoration.

Adoration means the act or process of adoring God for His many attributes such as His faithfulness, love and mercy, etc. Praising Him is one means of releasing His power. The following Psalms reflect some of King David's praises that illustrate adoration:

Psalm 27:4
"One thing I asked of the Lord,
    that will I seek after:
to live in the house of the Lord
    all the days of my life,
to behold the beauty of the Lord,
    and to inquire in his temple." (ESV)

Psalm 63:2-5
"So I have looked upon you in the sanctuary,
    beholding your power and glory.
Because your steadfast love is better than life,
    my lips will praise you.
So I will bless you as long as I live;
    in your name I will lift up my hands.
My soul will be satisfied as with fat and rich food,
    and my mouth will praise you with joyful lips." (ESV)

Psalm 73:25-26

"Whom have I in heaven but you?
 And there is nothing on earth that I desire
besides you.
 My flesh and my heart may fail,
but God is the strength[a] of my heart and my
 portion forever." (ESV)

Psalm 84:1–2

"How lovely is your dwelling place,
 O Lord of hosts!
My soul longs, yes, faints
 for the courts of the Lord;
my heart and my flesh sing for joy
 to the living God." (ESV)

Psalm 103:1-5

"Bless the Lord, O my soul,
 and all that is within me, bless his holy name.
Bless the Lord, O my soul,
 and forget not all his benefits,
who forgives all your iniquity,
 who heals all your diseases,
who redeems your life from the pit,
 who crowns you with steadfast love and mercy,
who satisfies you with good so that your
 youth is renewed like the eagle's." (ESV)

C - Confession

1 John 1:9 states, *"If we confess our sins, He is faithful and just to forgive us our sins, and cleanse us from unrighteousness."* (NKJV)

We need to confess our sins to God. The best format I know is the SINCERE format explained below:

"S"
"I"   }   **SIN** describe your sin in detail
"N"

"C" — Confess your motive in sinning

"E" — Explain the hurt caused

"R" — Repent of your behavior

"E" — Explain your offense to God

The following is Psalm 51:1-17, David's confession: To the choirmaster. A Psalm of David, when Nathan the prophet came to him after he had gone in to Bathsheba.

> *"Have mercy on me, O God,*
> *according to your steadfast love;*
> *according to your abundant mercy*
> *blot out my transgressions.*
> *Wash me thoroughly from my iniquity,*
> *and cleanse me from my sin.*
> *"For I know my transgressions,*
> *and my sin is ever before me.*
> *Against you, you alone, have I sinned,*
> *and done what is evil in your sight,*
> *so that you are justified in your sentence*

and blameless when you pass judgment.
Indeed, I was born guilty,
*   a sinner when my mother conceived me.*
"You desire truth in the inward being;
*   therefore teach me wisdom in my secret heart.*
Purge me with hyssop, and I shall be clean;
*   wash me, and I shall be whiter than snow.*
Let me hear joy and gladness;
*   let the bones that you have crushed rejoice.*
Hide your face from my sins,
*   and blot out all my iniquities.*
"Create in me a clean heart, O God,
*   and put a new and right spirit within me.*
Do not cast me away from your presence,
*   and do not take your Holy Spirit from me.*
Restore to me the joy of your salvation,
*   and sustain in me a willing spirit.*
Then I will teach transgressors your ways,
*   and sinners will return to you.*
Deliver me from bloodshed, O God,
*   O God of my salvation,*
*   and my tongue will sing aloud of your deliverance.*
"O Lord, open my lips,
*   and my mouth will declare your praise.*
For you have no delight in sacrifice;
*   if I were to give a burnt offering, you would not*
be pleased.

The sacrifice acceptable to God is a broken spirit;
*   a broken and contrite heart, O God, you will not*
despise."

T - Thanksgiving

Go to God with a Grateful Attitude.

Without thankfulness, we can become arrogant and self-centered. By meditating on all the good things that God has done for us, we can develop a thankful heart. If we have a sour attitude, then we cannot be grateful, and therefore our relationship with God is not right. When we have a thankful heart and spirit, we have joy, and when we have joy we will be able to be a witness to all the good things that God has done for us, and we will share that with others and glorify God. John 15:11 says, *"These things have I spoken unto you, that My joy might remain in you and that your joy might be full."* This is the joy of abiding!

The following is Psalm 100:

> *"Make a joyful noise to the Lord, all the earth.*
>   *Worship the Lord with gladness;*
>   *come into his presence with singing.*
> *Know that the Lord is God.*
>   *It is he that made us, and we are his;*
>   *we are his people, and the sheep of his pasture.*
> *Enter his gates with thanksgiving,*
>   *and his courts with praise.*
>   *Give thanks to him, bless his name.*
> *For the Lord is good;*
>   *his steadfast love endures forever,*
>   *and his faithfulness to all generations."*

S - Supplication

Supplication is a noun that comes from the Latin verb *supplicare*, which means "to plead humbly." While a **supplication** is often thought of as a religious prayer (it is used 60 times in the **Bible**), it can logically be applied to any situation in which you must entreat someone in power for help or a favor.

A very important acrostic I learned many years ago is J-O-Y—Jesus first, others second, yourself last.

The following are some supplication prayers:

> **Psalm 4:1**
> *"Answer me when I call, O God of my right!*
> *You gave me room when I was in distress.*
> *Be gracious to me, and hear my prayer."*

> **Psalm 6:4**
> *"Turn, O Lord, save my life;*
> *deliver me for the sake of your steadfast love."*

> **Psalm 7:1**
> *"O Lord my God, in you I take refuge;*
> *save me from all my pursuers, and deliver me,"*

> **Psalm 119:170**
> *"Let my supplication come before you;*
> *deliver me according to your promise."*

Abiding

The word abiding means continuing for a long time: enduring, such as an abiding interest in nature. As stated by Jesus in John Chapter 15, He explains how the branches can only bear fruit if they abide in the vine, so the only way that we (believers) can glorify the Father is through having fruitful lives by abiding in the Trinity (God, Christ, and the Holy Spirit).

We have been considering the ACTS formula for a complete prayer. It's an excellent format and has endured through the years, but I need to say some things about keeping the main thing the main thing. First and foremost, effective prayer is all about an intimate relationship with our Heavenly Father, God, through the inspiration of His Holy Spirit as you "hang out" with each other all day, every day. Without a relationship with God, our prayers are offered in vain. THIS IS THE MOST IMPORTANT TEACHING IN THIS ENTIRE BOOK, SO WE COVERED IT ONE MORE TIME!

From Chapter 6 – *Criteria for God's Rewards* – CROWN, we will see that whoever prays for the praise of men will receive it – from men – but there will be no reward from God. In other words, God only blesses that which occurs because of abiding in Him. To abide in Him then is to be in a wholeheartedly obedient relationship with Him. In New Testament terms, we are to be slaves to Him – one hundred percent obedient to Him from a love motive!

A favorite motivational verse for me through the years has been Isaiah 6:8, *"And I heard the voice of the Lord saying, "Whom shall I send, and who will go for us?" Then I said, "Here am I! Send me."* (ESV)

My life verse (personalized), Ezra 7:10: *"For Ezra* (John George) *had set his heart to study the law of the Lord, and to do it, and to teach his statutes and ordinances in Israel."* (Liberty University)

If you haven't come to the point in your walk with God that you have a life verse, I encourage you to find a verse that motivates you to a higher calling.

Theme: John 15:11 – *"I have said these things to you so that my joy may be in you, and that your joy may be complete."*

CHAPTER 4
Bible Study
Who, What, When,
Where, How, Why

"All Scripture is God-breathed and is useful for teaching, rebuking, correcting and training in righteousness, so that the servant of God[a] may be thoroughly equipped for every good work." 2 Timothy 3:16-17 (ESV)

Growth in the Christian life occurs as the Christian matures through his study of God's Word, abiding moment by moment with the Holy Spirit. The following "Bible Study Tool Box" has guided my study of the Bible through the years. Make a copy, keep it in your Bible, and use it! But first, why should you study God's Word?

Psalm 19:7-11

"The law of the Lord is perfect,
  reviving the soul;
the decrees of the Lord are sure,
  making wise the simple;
the precepts of the Lord are right,
  rejoicing the heart;
the commandment of the Lord is clear,
  enlightening the eyes;
the fear of the Lord is pure,
  enduring forever;
the ordinances of the Lord are true
  and righteous altogether.
More to be desired are they than gold,
  even much fine gold;
sweeter also than honey,
  and drippings of the honeycomb.
Moreover by them is your servant warned;
  in keeping them there is great reward."

The Christian's Call and Election – 2 Peter 1:3-4

"His divine power has given us everything needed for life and godliness, through the knowledge of him who called us by his own glory and goodness. Thus he has given us, through these things, his precious and very great promises, so that through them you may escape from the

corruption that is in the world because of lust, and may become participants of the divine nature."

"BIBLE STUDY TOOL BOX"

"Open my eyes, so that I may behold wondrous things out of your law."

Psalm 119:18

We have five ways of consuming God's Word; we hear it, read it, study it, memorize it and meditate on it.

5 Means of Taking in God's Word
Hear, Read, Study, Memorize Meditate

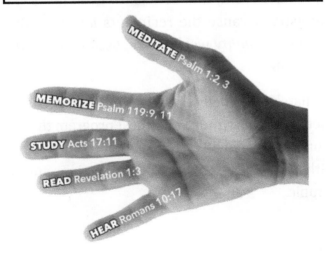

"BIBLE STUDY TOOL BOX"
Continued

---

7 Rules of Bible Study and Interpretation
Acrostic: **DEF GHIJ**
3 Study the Bible Rules

D **D**evotionally: profound dedication; consecration

E **E**xpectantly: to look for with reason and justification

F **F**aithfully: reliable, trusted, and believed

4 Interpret the Bible Rules

G **G**rammatically: must not violate the known usage of a word or invent another which has no precedent

H **H**istorically: must have awareness of the life and society of the times in which the Scripture was written

I **I**mmediate/Wider Context: the meaning must be gathered from the context

J **J**ointly with other Scripture: Interpret unclear passages in Scripture in light of the clear one

---

Here are a couple of other relevant factors. The first is faith; God said it, I believe it, that settles it! Even Jesus was limited in His ministry because the recipients lacked faith: *"And he did not do many mighty works there, because of their unbelief."* Matthew 13:58

Immediately after being saved in June of 1961 on Okinawa I began memorizing Scripture. The best program that I am aware of is the one illustrated on page 63. As you can see, it is a topical study with twelve verses in each of five sections and two verses on each topic.

"BIBLE STUDY TOOL BOX"
Continued

3 Steps to Analyzing a Bible Passage

Step 1: **Observation**: What does the passage say?
Step 2: **Interpretation**: What does the passage mean?
Step 3: **Application**: How am I going to apply what the passage says and means to my life?

Step 1: OBSERVATION - What Does It Say?
Acrostic: ME CE IC R C P C

ME	MEANS - END	"if...then"	2 Chronicles 7:14
CE	CAUSE - EFFECT	"Therefore" or "because (of)"	Jeremiah 3:1-3
IC	INTRODUCTION - CONCLUSION	Look for a difference and determine why	Compare: Romans1:18 with 5:1 See wrath vs peace Romans 3:21-31
R	REPEATED WORDS	Phrases or ideas	1 John 4:7-8
C	COMPARISON	Simile (like, as)	Psalm 1:1
P	PROGRESSION	"and" or "than"	see Mark's Gospel (nearly every verse)
C	CONTRAST	"but"	Galatians 5:13-26

Step 2: INTERPRETATION - What Does It Mean?
What - When - Where - How - Why

Rudyard Kipling said, "I keep six honest serving-men (They taught me all I knew); Their names are What and Why and When and How and Where and Who. "

Step 3: APPLICATION - How Does It Apply?
Acrostic: SPACE TRUST

S	SIN	Is there a SIN to avoid?	**T**	TEACH	What does the passage TEACH?
P	PROMISE	a PROMISE to claim?	**R**	RELATIONSHIP	to my RELATIONSHIP with God or others?
A	ATTITUDE	an ATTITUDE to change?	**U**	UNDERSTANDING	to UNDERSTANDING God, self or others?
C	COMMAND	a COMMAND to obey?	**S**	SHARE	that I should SHARE with others?
E	EXAMPLE	an EXAMPLE to follow?	**T**	TIMELESS PRINCIPLES	in applying TIMELESS PRINCIPLES?

The first section, Living The New Life, identifies the six major areas the new Christian should begin developing.

The second section identifies the six major areas that should be used in leading others to Christ.

The third section outlines the significant resources available to all God's people. These verses have encouraged me now for more than 57 years – trust me!

The fourth section provides guidance on our mission to make disciples, but first, we must be a disciple.

The fifth section focuses on the need to continually grow in Christlikeness; love, humility, purity, honesty, faith, and good works. Again, the verses recommended have been such a blessing. Of course, freely add favorites of your choice.

Navigator Topical Memory System (TMS)

LIVING THE NEW LIFE

Christ the Center	❏ 2 Corinthians 5:17	❏ Galatians 2:20
Obedience to Christ	❏ Romans 12:1	❏ John 14:21
The Word	❏ 2 Timothy 3:16	❏ Joshua 1:8
Prayer	❏ John 15:7	❏ Philippians 4:6, 7
Fellowship	❏ Matthew 18:20	❏ Hebrews 10:24, 25
Witnessing	❏ Matthew 4:19	❏ Romans 1:16

PROCLAIMING CHRIST

All Have Sinned	❏ Romans 3:23	❏ Isaiah 53:6
Sin's Penalty	❏ Romans 6:23	❏ Hebrews 9:27
Christ Paid the Penalty	❏ Romans 5:8	❏ 1 Peter 3:18
Salvation Not by Works	❏ Ephesians 2:8, 9	❏ Titus 3:5
Must Receive Christ	❏ John 1:12	❏ Revelation 3:20
Assurance of Salvation	❏ 1 John 5:13	❏ John 5:24

RELIANCE ON GOD'S RESOURCES

His Spirit	❏ 1 Corinthians 3:16	❏ 1 Corinthians 2:12
His Strength	❏ Isaiah 41:10	❏ Philippians 4:13
His Faithfulness	❏ Lamentations 3:22, 23	❏ Numbers 23:19
His Peace	❏ Isaiah 26:3	❏ 1 Peter 5:7
His Provision	❏ Romans 8:32	❏ Philippians 4:19
His Help in Temptation	❏ Hebrews 2:18	❏ Psalm 119:9, 11

BEING CHRIST'S DISCIPLE

Put Christ First	❏ Matthew 6:33	❏ Luke 9:23
Separate From the World	❏ 1 John 2:15,16	❏ Romans 12:2
Be Steadfast	❏ 1 Corinthians 15:58	❏ Hebrews 12:3
Serve Others	❏ Mark 10:45	❏ 2 Corinthians 4:5
Give Generously	❏ Proverbs 3:9,10	❏ 2 Corinthians 9:6,7
Develop World Vision	❏ Acts 1:8	❏ Matthew 28:19,20

GROWTH IN CHRISTLIKENESS

Love	❏ John 13:34,35	❏ 1 John 3:18
Humility	❏ Philippians 2:3,4	❏ 1 Peter 5:5,6
Purity	❏ Ephesians 5:3	❏ 1 Peter 2:11
Honesty	❏ Leviticus 19:11	❏ Acts 24:16
Faith	❏ Hebrews 11:6	❏ Romans 4:20,21
Good Works	❏ Galatians 6:9,10	❏ Matthew 5:16

Leading and Conducting Group Bible Studies

One of the most exciting and rewarding activities in all of Christendom today is the group Bible Study. As the name implies, it is a group of people who meet to read and study God's Word. Beyond that, it is virtually impossible to define further. For example, it may be three men who meet every Wednesday morning at their church from 6-7 a.m. or ten couples that meet once a week from 7-9 p.m. in their respective homes. The topics discussed may be book studies or topical studies over the full range of human experience. Participants may be old friends or a grouping from a "sign-up" list. Participants may share in leadership and teaching or follow an appointed teacher. In some cases, a designated leader may choose the topic, or the whole group may select it.

Bottom Line: There is no one right way to conduct a Group Bible Study.

Pray and Plan

A very successful method I have used for over fifty years to pick the topic to be studied is called the "Pray and Plan." As the name implies, this method involves two major activities – Praying and Planning. Not only are these two activities critical, but the sequence is also critical. Someone once said, "There may be something more important you can do after you have prayed, but there is nothing more important you can do until you have prayed." Regretfully, we make plans of what we want to do and then ask God to bless them. Done correctly, we ask God what

He would have us do, and we then make plans to accomplish His desire for us.

Conducting a Group Bible Study

The key word to keep in mind for those teaching or holding a Bible Study is spiritual maturity, yours and that of the group. If you are the leader and considerably more mature than the others, it is best for you to teach the study. In the former situation, you are considered the teacher. In the latter, you are more the facilitator. In both cases, the Bible Study Tool Box presented in this chapter provides the format to follow. Again, in the former situation, you teach it. In the latter, you facilitate its development drawing on the knowledge and experiences of those present.

NOTE: Many of the participants will have Study Bibles that have notes and outlines that have been added in by top Bible scholars, make sure you use them.

The following is an example of a teaching format for Hebrews 1:1-4 utilizing the Tool Box format:

I. Introduction

A. **Overview.** Today, I'll be introducing the Book of Hebrews, a book with an unusual "history" of its own. We'll also consider an overview of the book itself and my goal for each of us as we go through it.

B. Preview. Following the overview topics mentioned previously, we'll begin Hebrews today by discussing the first four verses of Chapter 1.

II. Lesson

A. **Background Information:** Who, What, When, Where, How, and Why?

B. **Big Idea:** Men and women receive the full revelation of God through Jesus Christ, and He alone enables them to enter into the very presence of God. In Jesus, God entered humanity, eternity has invaded time, and things can never be the same again.

C. **Outline of Hebrews:**

Chapters	*Title*
1	Christ, the Son of God
2 – 3	Christ, the Son of Man
4 -10	Christ, the High Priest
11 – 13	Christ, the Better Way
1:1 – 4:16	The Superiority of the Person of Christ
5:1 – 10:39	The Superiority of the Priesthood of Christ
11:1 – 13:19	The Superiority of the Power of Christ
13:20 – 13:25	Concluding Remarks

D. Read the Verse Aloud: Christ, Superior to the Prophets Hebrews 1:1-4

"Long ago God spoke to our ancestors in many and various ways by the prophets, but in these last days, he has spoken to us by a Son, whom he appointed heir of all things, through whom he also created the world. He is the reflection of God's glory and the exact imprint of God's very being, and he sustains all things by his powerful word. When he had made purification for sins, he sat down at the right hand of the Majesty on high, having become as much superior to angels as the name he has inherited is more excellent than theirs." (HCSB)

E. Now Break Down the Verses for Discussion:

1. **Verse 1:** *"Long ago, at many times and in many ways, God spoke to our fathers by the prophets;"*

2. **Verse 2:** *"but in these last days he has spoken to us by a Son, whom he appointed heir of all things, through whom he also created the world."*

3. **Verse 3:** *"He is the reflection of God's glory and the exact imprint of God's very being, and he sustains all things by his powerful word. When he had made purification for sins, he sat down at the right hand of the Majesty on high,"*

4. **Verse 4:** *"having become as much superior to angels as the name he has inherited is more excellent than theirs."*

III. Discussion

A. Does the ambiguity surrounding Hebrews affect your acceptance of it?

B. What role do the prophets play in the outworking of God's plan for His people?

C. What is the difference in the words from prophets verses and the words of Jesus?

D. Discuss the implications of Christ as *"He is the radiance of the glory of God and the exact imprint of his nature, and he upholds the universe by the word of his power."* Hebrews 1:3

IV. Truth Personalized:

S P A C E   T R U S T

Bible Verse APPLICATION - How Does It Apply?					
Application Key: SPACE TRUST					
S SIN	Is there a SIN to avoid?	**T**	TEACH	What does the passage TEACH?
P PROMISE	a PROMISE to claim?	**R**	RELATIONSHIP	about my RELATIONSHIP with God or others?
A ATTITUDE	an ATTITUDE to change?	**U**	UNDERSTANDING	about UNDERSTANDING of God, self or others?
C COMMAND	a COMMAND to obey?	**S**	SHARE	that I should SHARE with others
E EXAMPLE	an EXAMPLE to follow?	**T**	TIMELESS PRINCIPLES	that are TIMELESS PRINCIPLES?

My specific application for this week is _____

_____.

NEXT WEEK'S LESSON: HEBREWS 1:5-14

MY GOAL FOR EACH OF US IN THIS STUDY: THAT DAY-BY-DAY, EACH OF US WOULD **SEE** CHRIST MORE CLEARLY, **LOVE** CHRIST MORE DEARLY AND **FOLLOW** CHRIST MORE NEARLY.

Bible Study Resources

Whether you are teaching, facilitating or simply attending a Bible Study, it is imperative that you find good Bible study resources since these are critical for accurate study. An excellent Study Bible is a great place to begin – there are at least 60 versions of the Bible in the English language. Additional resources can be found in church libraries, Christian bookstores, and there's a whole new world with computer resources. On the Internet there is a fantastic site entitled "Bible Gateway," which would give you answers or enhance your study by typing in a few words of a familiar passage or give you other desired biblical information.

Bible Study Evaluation

Although I have rarely seen it done, a very profitable activity at the conclusion of a Bible Study would be to evaluate its effectiveness. What is it that we did well? What should we keep doing? Or what could we do more of? What did we not do well that we should fix or stop doing altogether? Finally, were there things we did not do that we should have done? How effective were we in attaining our goals?

CHAPTER 5
A Proven Christian Values Dating System

Dating That Honors God

n this chapter I have used an outline format in order to give you a lot of information organized in a form that will be easier for you to remember.

I. Introduction

    A. Marriage today is an endangered species!

    B. Background – See Acknowledgments in this chapter; Take your shoes off – this is HOLY GROUND!

    C. ROOT CAUSES of problems in relationships:

1. Our MINDS have been CONFORMED to the world system and not to the LORD. Further, for most of us, they are CONFUSED concerning appropriate dating behavior by a society (world system), which is PLURALISTIC, DYNAMIC and FALLEN.

2. Our EMOTIONS have been CHARGED by internal and external stimuli and long for expression. Further, for many of us, our emotions have been DAMAGED by previous physical and/or verbal abuse, the implications of which are serious and pervasive.

3. Our WILLS have been WEAKENED by our past failures and our ever-present DESIRE to please ourselves and/or others rather than the LORD.

D. Sources of Decisions and The Battle Within

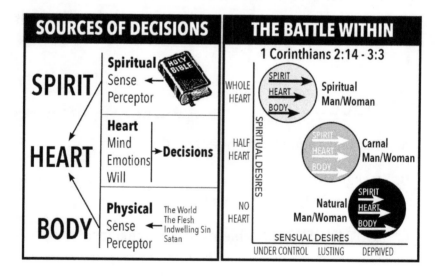

E. WHO NEEDS THIS? For the reasons stated above (and others), ALL Christians need a COMMON VALUE SYSTEM that honors God in all our relationships, especially those involving dating, engagement, and marriage.

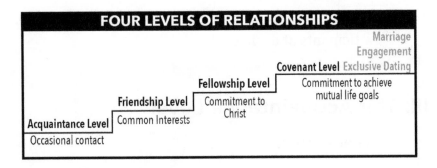

II. Proposed Four Levels Model

A. Two Foundational Rules That Govern The Model

1. **In a relationship, the NATURE OF THE COMMU-NICATION (depth of sharing, physical expression, etc.) should be determined by the LEVEL of the relationship.**

2. **The level of the relationship should be determined by the individuals' COMMITMENT TO CHRIST, and by their COMMITMENT TO MUTUAL LIFE GOALS.**

B. Strengths of Proposed Model

1. Based upon SCRIPTURAL PRINCIPLES

2. Reflects CONTEMPORARY CULTURE within God's absolutes

3. Recognizes that there are DIFFERENT LEVELS of relationships

4. Acknowledges that DIFFERENT TYPES OF COMMUNICATION are appropriate for each level of relationship

5. Identifies FREEDOMS and RESPONSIBILITIES of participants at each level

III. The Acquaintance Level

A. Characteristics:

1. Based upon – OCCASIONAL CONTACT – FREEDOM TO – ASK GENERAL QUESTIONS.

2. Duty – BE SENSITIVE TO THEIR NEEDS. The individuals you have contact with may or may not be Christian. Keep in mind that those who do not have Christ will spend eternity in hell. Let your light shine! Following are references to our greatest Call, Commandment, and Commission: Matthew 11:28-30; 22:37-40; 28:19-20.

B. Relevant questions concerning the Acquaintance Level:

1. Is there such a thing as love at first sight? Answer: No, it's infatuation, not love.

    Infatuation: in – INTENSITY + fatuous = FOOLISH or INANE, ESPECIALLY IN AN UNCONSCIOUS, COMPLACENT MANNER; SILLY.

Properly viewed: LOVE IS A SKILL TO BE LEARNED. 1 Corinthians 13:4-8a

2. Is it wrong to be emotionally attracted to another? Answer: No! God created us to be attracted to the opposite sex.

   The PROBLEM is it is tremendously OVEREMPHASIZED and ABUSED.

3. What part does physical appearance play? Answer: TOO MUCH!

   Physical beauty is a CULTURAL phenomenon.

   Emphasizing BEAUTY (or any other TEMPORARY quality) will cause ANXIETY.

   Instead, emphasis should be placed on one's CHARACTER.

4. What is appropriate at this level? One should focus on being sensitive to and meeting the needs of one's acquaintance's in the hope that your caring will lead to opportunities to share your faith in Christ.

IV. The Friendship Level

A. Characteristics:

   1. Based upon – COMMON INTERESTS

   2. Freedom to – ASK SPECIFIC QUESTIONS – 3 F'S: Family, Future, Faith

3. Duty to – ENCOURAGE PERSONAL GROWTH. Be committed to other's success. Always seek win-win relationships

B. Relevant question: Is it OK for a Christian to date a non-Christian? Answer: NO

The rationale for the "no" answer is its potential for becoming unequally yoked: *"Do not be unequally yoked with unbelievers. For what partnership has righteousness with lawlessness? Or what fellowship has light with darkness?"* 2 Corinthians 6:14 (ESV)

THE PRINCIPLE HERE IS THAT COMMON VALUES ARE ESSENTIAL IN A DATING RELATIONSHIP!

C. What is appropriate at this level? The same as the Acquaintance Level but this can now be done on a more personal level as you specifically inquire about your friend's family, future, and faith.

V. The Fellowship Level

A. Characteristics:

1. Based upon: COMMITMENT TO CHRIST – 1 John 1:3-7

2. Freedom to: SUGGEST PERSONAL GROWTH PROJECTS

3 Duty to: ENCOURAGE SPIRITUAL GROWTH. The scriptural 29 *"One-Another's"* define our duties to all Christian relationships.

B. Relevant questions:

1. What constitutes a DATE? Answer: A SOCIAL AP-POINTMENT WITH A PERSON OF THE OPPOSITE SEX TO BUILD THEM UP IN CHRIST.

REASONS to support the proposed definition.

    a. Gives us a GOAL for dating, but retains CREATIVITY.

    b. Provides CRITERIA for evaluation.

    c. Stresses the fact that NO ROMANCE is implied.

    d. Points those dating to the 29 SCRIPTURAL "ONE ANOTHERS."

    e. Limits PHYSICAL and EMOTIONAL freedom to achieve the goal.

2. When is an individual ready to date? Answer: WHEN YOU ARE A CHRISTIAN AND HAVE ATTAINED THE FOLLOWING MINIMAL QUALIFICATIONS:

    a. You understand the SERIOUSNESS of dating (See below).

    b. You have PERSONALLY worked out dating standards from Scripture.

    c. You are COMMITTED to following these standards without compromise.

    d. When there is evidence you are working toward an INDEPENDENT LEVEL of maturity in three areas: Physical, Financial, and especially Emotional.

3. What about GROUP DATING? Answer: It's GREAT for the following reasons:

    a. Allows the relationship to develop MORE SLOWLY.

    b. Great environment for learning SOCIAL SKILLS.

    c. Allows WOMEN to initiate activities.

    d. Reminds us of the need for OPENNESS in our dating.

    e. Enhances the probability you'll marry your BEST FRIEND!

4. How should one initiate a date? Answer: Remember the definition – have a SPECIFIC PLAN in mind. Do it with CLASS and RESPECT for the proposed date.

5. Why should one say "No" to dating invitations?

    a. The man is NOT A CHRISTIAN or NOT WALKING with Christ.

    b. The woman does NOT KNOW the man well enough to feel comfortable alone with him.

6. How should the man respond to the answer "No" for a dating invitation?

    a. If the woman has an EXTREMELY BUSY SCHEDULE, then propose an alternative time.

    b. The woman does NOT have to give a reason – DON'T PUSH!

7. What does it mean to DEFRAUD someone? Answer: TO RAISE EXPECTATIONS WHICH CANNOT BE RIGHTEOUSLY FULFILLED – 1 Thessalonians 4:3-8. A key here is the overriding PRINCIPLE of DEFERENCE: Limiting my freedom for the sake of someone else. Romans 14:19-23

   a. Flirting. (From French – *flower-to-flower*) – EYES – FLATTERY – TEASING. In reality, flirting is PLAYING at love without accepting the COMMITMENT or the RESPONSIBILITY of the relationship.

   b. Dress. This is the PRIMARY WAY women defraud men because men are "wired" for this (most pornography sold to men) – LOW TOPS – LOW JEANS – TIGHT CLOTHES – SKIN. The question is: Where will a man's FOCUS be drawn – to your BODY or your COUNTENANCE? Fellows too: Tight PANTS & short SHORTS – Same: body or countenance? Both: Form-fitting clothes.

   c. The frequency of interaction. BOTH must guard this one; it's the DOUBLE message that's the problem here. It is SAYING you're not serious, but ACTING otherwise.

   d. Sharing DEEPEST personal problems versus sharing with other fellows, or women sharing with other women. CAUTION: Be very careful men not to use the intimacy and spiritual aspect of prayer to defraud women, by your words or tone, when praying together.

    e. Jealousy/moodiness. Evidence of IMMATURITY (see Fruit of the Spirit), the need is to hold each other with an "OPEN HAND" as evidence of trust in God.

    f. Physical involvement. HUGS – KISSES – BACK RUBS – WRESTLING – PETTING. The PRINCIPLE OF DEFERENCE is particularly critical here as is RATIONALIZATION.

7. What are some GUIDELINES for dating that you would suggest? Answer:

"G" — GO very, very slowly.

"U" — Be UNCOMPROMISING in your scriptural standards.

"I" — INTERNAL thought life must be guarded and controlled.

"D" — DON'T fantasize sexually or otherwise.

"E" — EXIT vulnerable situations immediately; better yet, avoid them!

"L" — LEARN alternative ways of expressing love (see *Five Languages of Love* by Gary Chapman)

"I" — IF sex is not given a foothold; other areas will develop.

"N" — NEVER rationalize.

"E" — _____ (YOUR CHOICE!)

VI. The Covenant Level

A. Characteristics:

    1. Based upon: COMMITMENT TO ACHIEVE MUTUAL LIFE GOALS

    2. Freedom to: CORRECT EACH OTHER

    3. Duty to: ENCOURAGE TOTAL GROWTH IN THE AREA OF COMMITMENT. Again, the *29 Scriptural One-Another's* define our duties here. Since they apply to all Christian relationships, HOW MUCH MORE SO TO OUR DEEPEST RELATIONSHIPS OF EXCLUSIVE DATING, ENGAGEMENT, AND MARRIAGE, which should reflect in growing measure the relationship between Christ and the church! Ephesians 5:22-33

B. Relevant question: Are there other covenant relationships other than dating ones? Answer: Yes! If you're a member of a sports team, singing group, have a job, etc., each of these is a covenant relationship. When you take a class, the syllabus establishes a covenant relationship with the professor. So, all of us are in many covenant relationships.

VII. Exclusive Dating Relationship – Goal: One In Spirit

A. DEFINITION. A covenant agreement between a man and a woman not to date others in order (1) to deepen their relationship, and (2) to seek God's will concerning marriage.

NOTE: "...to deepen their relationship" DOES NOT MEAN PHYSICALLY. If your dating relationship up to this point has been more physical than spiritual, you have developed habits, which are DYSFUNCTIONAL to developing a lasting relationship! Two characteristics about the NATURE OF SEX play havoc with the "good intentions" of couples:

1. Sex is progressive. It's like a toboggan ride. It is difficult to go back to previous arousal levels and tends to push the physical level of the relationship beyond the couple's level of commitment. Sexual arousal was intended by God for marriage: 1 Thessalonians 4:3-8; 1 Corinthians 6:9-20. Once begun, there are just two alternatives: guilt or frustration.

2. Sex is dominant. Once let on the stage, it steals the whole show! It dominates everything else until the novelty is gone. It takes little effort but is extremely intense.

B. Making Righteous Decisions. The 1 Corinthians 6:12-20 passage provides three guidelines for making moral decisions. Consider the following three questions concerning types of dating (or other) behavior: Is it beneficial? (v.12); Is it enslaving? (v. 12); Is it glorifying to God? (v.20)

C. Recognize the DANGER.

1. Of DRIFTING into this level of relationship. CAUTION: Don't assume there is a commitment. IF IT HAS NOT BEEN VERBALIZED, ASK!

2. Of COMMUNICATING (verbally or physically) on this level without having made the COMMITMENT and accepted the RESPONSIBILITY.

D. Relevant question: When is an individual ready to date exclusively? Answer: When you have attained all of the criteria outlined in The Fellowship Level on page 77 (under V-B-2), and there is evidence that you are achieving the INTERDEPENDENT LEVEL of maturity. Further, there is evidence that you are committed to glorifying Christ in all of your relationships, you are in obedience to the authorities of your life (parental, school, work), and your parents know the boy/girl and approve of the relationship.

> CAUTION: Any evidence of rebellion in the practice of the *29 One Another's* or in the adoption of the world's principles should be seen as "yellow" or "red" flags concerning the soundness of your relationship. Independence includes three major areas: physical, financial, and emotional. Be assured that if relationships with parents are broken or damaged, you will experience additional problems in your marriage. This is especially true of a daughter's relationship with her father and a son's relationship with his mother. If this is your situation, determine to mend it/them BEFORE you enter the covenant level relationships, especially engagement and marriage!

E. What is APPROPRIATE BEHAVIOR for this level of relationship? Answer:

1. Discuss MARRIAGE (values and life goals).

2. PRAY together on a regular basis.

3. Establish a relationship with godly COUPLES.

4. Spend FREQUENT and REGULAR time together.

5. READ an excellent Christian book on marriage.

6. Get to know each other's PARENTS.

7. LIMIT physical expression.

8. Discuss the PAST before engagement (with sensitivity!)

F. What is INAPPROPRIATE BEHAVIOR for this level of relationship? Answer:

1. ASSUMING engagement and marriage will follow.

2. Extensive PHYSICAL expression.

F. TWO IMPORTANT NOTES.

1. To COUPLES entering an Exclusive Dating Relationship: DO NOT HIDE IT FROM OTHERS – they need to see models of godly relationships.

2. To OBSERVERS of Exclusive Dating Relationships: DO NOT pressure them into marriage. God may want to lead them out of the relationship, so make it easy for them to listen to God. DON'T YOU PLAY GOD!

VIII. Engagement – Goal: One In Spirit and One In Soul

    A. DEFINITION. A covenant agreement between a man and a woman not to date others (1) to prepare for marriage and (2) to see if God closes doors concerning marriage.

    B. What is APPROPRIATE BEHAVIOR for this level of relationship? Answer:

        1. CONTINUE to develop all of the previous areas.

        2. DEEPEN relationships with one or two godly couples.

        3. DEEPEN relationship with parents (honor them).

        4. Begin MARRIAGE COUNSELING.

        5. LIMITED physical expression.

        6. Make SPECIFIC marriage plans.

    C. What is INAPPROPRIATE BEHAVIOR for this level of relationship?

    Answer: Extensive physical contact

IX. Marriage – Goal: One In Spirit, Soul, and Body

    A. DEFINITION. A lifetime covenant agreement between a man and a woman to maintain a one-man-one-woman relationship, according to scriptural standards, for as long as they both shall live. Following is the traditional vow (covenant agreement):

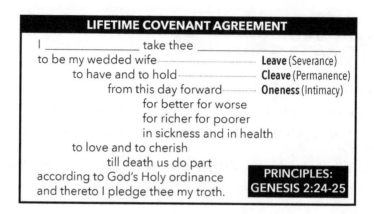

B. Genesis 2:18-25; Ephesians 5:16-33; 1 Peter 3:1-7—
   Principles for the Marriage Relationship

C. Watch out for substitutes (see The World's Principles for
   Marriage and Life chart, last chart in this Chapter):

   I love you because . . . .

   I love you if . . . .

   Competition instead of completion

X. Summary and Conclusion

*ACKNOWLEDGMENTS: Although it is impossible to credit
all those who have significantly influenced this teaching, the
following are specifically known: Pastor John White, IBLP, Paul
Little, Alan Redpath, Jerry Evans, my personal fifty-nine years of
marriage, two children, six grandchildren, one great-grandchild,
and over forty years in ministry on college campuses.

GOD'S PRINCIPLES FOR LIFE AND MARRIAGE

Loving God and Others (Matthew 11:28-30;22:37-40: 28:19-20)					
Genesis 1:26-28 **Love and Obedience (Being)**			**Genesis 1:26-28; Ephesians 5:22-33; 1 Peter 3:1-7** **Love and Submission (Honoring)**		
Principle	Symptom	Result	Principle	Symptom	Result
Reflect	Personal Worth in Christ	Security	Severance	Leave	Independence
Reign	Meaningful Activity (Life=Ministry)	Significance	Permanence	Cleave	Interdependence
Reproduce	Meaningful Relationship (Good Samaritan)	Love	Unity	Oneness	Intimacy

WORLD'S PRINCIPLES FOR LIFE AND MARRIAGE

Self-Love (Me Oriented Substitutes) (Judges 21:25)					
Judges 14:1-3; James 4:1-4 **Internal Substitutes for Love (Responding)**			**Proverbs 29:18; John 2:15-16** **External Substitutes for Life (Having)**		
Principle	Symptom	Result	Principle	Symptom	Result
I Love You "Because"	Focus on Weakness	Poor Self-Esteem	Success	Over-Committed	Surface Gains but Root Pains
I Love You "If..."	Focus on Performance	Rebellion or Indifference	If My Needs Met	No Real Commitments	Great Instability
Competition not Completion	Frustration and Loneliness	Both Lose (Divorce)	Vicarious Stimulation	Sexy Clothes Pornography Adultery	Disunity and Bondage

CHAPTER 6
God's Rewards
C.R.O.W.N.

Eternal Rewards

1. "C" Commitment/ Faithfulness

Matthew 25:14-30 Concerning Our Talents and Abilities

"For it is as if a man, going on a journey, summoned his slaves and entrusted his property to them; to one he gave five talents, to another two, to another one, to each according to his ability. Then he went away.

The one who had received the five talents went off at once and traded with them, and made five more talents. In the same way, the one who had the two talents made two more talents. But the one who had received the one talent went off and dug a hole in the ground and hid his master's money.

After a long time, the master of those slaves came and settled accounts with them. Then the one who had received the five talents came forward, bringing five more talents, saying, 'Master, you handed over to me five talents; see, I have made five more talents.' His master said to him, 'Well done, good and trustworthy slave; you have been trustworthy in a few things, I will put you in charge of many things; enter into the joy of your master.' And the one with the two talents also came forward, saying, 'Master, you handed over to me two talents; see, I have made two more talents.' His master said to him, 'Well done, good and trustworthy slave; you have been trustworthy in a few things, I will put you in charge of many things; enter into the joy of your master.' Then the one who had received the one talent also came forward, saying, 'Master, I knew that you were a harsh man, reaping where you did not sow, and gathering where you did not scatter seed; so I was afraid, and I went and hid your talent in the ground. Here you have what is yours.'

But his master replied, 'You wicked and lazy slave! You knew, did you, that I reap where I did not sow, and gather where I did not scatter? Then you ought to have invested my money with the bankers, and on my return, I would have received what was my own with interest. So take the talent from him, and give it to the one with the ten talents. For to all those who have, more will be provided, and they will have an abundance; but from those who have nothing, even what they have will be taken away. As for this worthless slave, throw him into the outer darkness, where there will be weeping and gnashing of teeth."

From the parable above we learn of a man going on a journey who entrusted money to his slaves, **each according to their ability,** with the understanding that they would invest it while he was gone. One got five talents, one two talents a third servant one talent and he decided to bury it. When the owner returned, he was pleased with the first two but furious with the one who had buried his. In fact, he took the one talent away that had been buried and gave it to the one who now had ten talents.

TRUST	RESULT	CAUTION	PRINCIPLE
5 & 2 & 1	5 + 5 + 1 2 + 2 1 − 1	Don't bury your trust	Be faithful with what God has given you

What are we to learn from this parable?

1. Different people have differing abilities

2. God expects results to mirror our abilities

3. Refusing to apply what God has entrusted to us is a rebellion against God

4. God withholds His blessing to those who bury their talents, those who are unfaithful and not committed

5. God gives different talents to different slaves according to their abilities, but He gave the same reward to those who had faithfully used what was given to them

2. "R" Reason/Motive

Matthew 6:1-18 Concerning Giving

"Beware of practicing your piety before others in order to be seen by them; for then you have no reward from your Father in heaven.

"So whenever you give alms, do not sound a trumpet before you, as the hypocrites do in the synagogues and in the streets, so that they may be praised by others. Truly I tell you, they have received their reward. But when you give alms, do not let your left hand know what your right hand is doing, so that your alms may be done in secret; and your Father who sees in secret will reward you".

Concerning Prayer

"And whenever you pray, do not be like the hypocrites; for they love to stand and pray in the synagogues and at the street corners, so that they may be seen by others. Truly I tell you, they have received their reward. But whenever you pray, go into your room and shut the door and pray to your Father who is in secret; and your Father who sees in secret will reward you."

"When you are praying, do not heap up empty phrases as the Gentiles do; for they think that they will be heard because of their many words. Do not be like them, for your Father knows what you need before you ask him.

"*Pray then in this way:*

Our Father in heaven,

hallowed be your name.

Your kingdom come.

Your will be done,

on earth as it is in heaven.

Give us this day our daily bread.

And forgive us our debts,

as we also have forgiven our debtors.

And do not bring us to the time of trial,

but rescue us from the evil one.

"*For if you forgive others their trespasses, your heavenly Father will also forgive you; but if you do not forgive others, neither will your Father forgive your trespasses.*"

Concerning Fasting

"*And whenever you fast, do not look dismal, like the hypocrites, for they disfigure their faces so as to show others that they are fasting. Truly I tell you, they have received their reward. But when you fast, put oil on your head and wash your face, so that your fasting may be seen not by others but by your Father who is in secret; and your Father who sees in secret will reward you.*"

	R – Reason/Motive		
TRUST	**RESULT**	**CAUTION**	**PRINCIPLE**
Acts to receive God's praise	Instead, men act to receive men's praise	Men's praise received, but NO reward from God	Seek God's praise, not man's

What are we to learn from these three Biblical passages?

1. God sees and judges all that we do in life

2. God desires that we glorify Him in all things

3. Seeking the praise of men for our giving to others, fasting or praying will result in the praise of men, but we will receive none from God!

4. Only that which is done for the praise of God will be rewarded by Him

3. "O" Opportunities

O - Opportunities Matthew 20:1-16

Matthew 20:1-16 - The Laborers in the Vineyard

"For the kingdom of heaven is like a landowner who went out early in the morning to hire laborers for his vineyard. After agreeing with the laborers for the usual daily wage, he sent them into his vineyard. When he went out about nine o'clock, he saw others standing idle in the marketplace; and he said to them, 'You also go into the vineyard, and I will pay you whatever is right.' So they

went. When he went out again about noon and about three o'clock, he did the same. And about five o'clock he went out and found others standing around; and he said to them, 'Why are you standing here idle all day?'

They said to him, 'Because no one has hired us.

' He said to them, 'You also go into the vineyard.'

When evening came, the owner of the vineyard said to his manager, 'Call the laborers and give them their pay, beginning with the last and then going to the first.'

When those hired about five o'clock came, each of them received the usual daily wage. Now when the first came, they thought they would get more; but each of them received the usual daily wage. And when they received it, they grumbled against the landowner, saying, 'These last worked only one hour, and you have made them equal to us who have borne the burden of the day and the scorching heat.'

But he replied to one of them, 'Friend, I am doing you no wrong; did you not agree with me for the usual daily wage? Take what belongs to you and go; I choose to give to this last the same as I give to you. Am I not allowed to do what I choose with what belongs to me? Or are you envious because I am generous?'

So the last will be first, and the first will be last."

TRUST	RESULT	CAUTION	PRINCIPLE
Our opportunities vary from person to person	Some people have less opportunity than others	Don't compare your opportunity with others Don't envy!	God blesses as He chooses

What are we to learn from these four Scriptures?

1. God rewards as He pleases considering the opportunities we have had, not what we call fairness

2. Don't envy others concerning what God gave them

3. God has the right to be generous to whom He chooses

4. God blesses as He wishes in this case more to those who had less opportunity

4. "W" Works Achieved

Luke 19:11-27 – Concerning How Much We Are Producing

"As they were listening to this, he went on to tell a parable, because he was near Jerusalem, and because they supposed that the kingdom of God was to appear immediately. So he said, "A nobleman went to a distant country to get royal power for himself and then return. He summoned ten of his slaves, and gave them ten pounds, and said to them, 'Do business with these until I come back.'

But the citizens of his country hated him and sent a delegation after him, saying, 'We do not want this man

to rule over us.' When he returned, having received royal power, he ordered these slaves, to whom he had given the money, to be summoned so that he might find out what they had gained by trading.

The first came forward and said, 'Lord, your pound has made ten more pounds.' He said to him, 'Well done, good slave! Because you have been trustworthy in a very small thing, take charge of ten cities.' Then the second came, saying, 'Lord, your pound has made five pounds.' He said to him, 'And you, rule over five cities.' Then the other came, saying, 'Lord, here is your pound. I wrapped it up in a piece of cloth, for I was afraid of you because you are a harsh man; you take what you did not deposit, and reap what you did not sow.'

He said to him, 'I will judge you by your own words, you wicked slave! You knew, did you, that I was a harsh man, taking what I did not deposit and reaping what I did not sow? Why then did you not put my money into the bank? Then when I returned, I could have collected it with interest.' He said to the bystanders, 'Take the pound from him and give it to the one who has ten pounds.' (And they said to him, 'Lord, he has ten pounds!')

'I tell you, to all those who have, more will be given; but from those who have nothing, even what they have will be taken away. But as for these enemies of mine who did not want me to be king over them—bring them here and slaughter them in my presence.'"

W – Works Achieved			
TRUST	**RESULT**	**CAUTION**	**PRINCIPLE**
Works achieved vary from person to person	Some people produce less than others, some more than others	Work hard at your job and produce as much as you can	God rewards hard work achievement and punishes no work

What are we to learn from these Scriptures?

1. God trusts us to bear a quantity of fruit in all that we do

2. God realizes that different people produce more than others

3. God blesses those who bear more fruit than others with more significant rewards

5. "N" Nature of Works Achieved (Quality)

1 Corinthians 3:10-15 – Concerning the Nature of Your Works as to Their Quality and Permanence

> *"According to the grace of God given to me, like a skilled master builder I laid a foundation, and someone else is building on it. Each builder must choose with care how to build on it. For no one can lay any foundation other than the one that has been laid; that foundation is Jesus Christ."*

> *"Now if anyone builds on the foundation with gold, silver, precious stones, wood, hay, straw— the work of*

each builder will become visible, for the Day will disclose it, because it will be revealed with fire, and the fire will test what sort of work each has done.

If what has been built on the foundation survives, the builder will receive a reward. If the work is burned up, the builder will suffer loss; the builder will be saved, but only as through fire."

N – Nature of Works Achieved (Quality)			
TRUST	**RESULT**	**CAUTION**	**PRINCIPLE**
The nature of our ministry is our choice	God's future praise and blessing or nothing!	The enemy of the best is not bad things, but good things that are not the best things	Invest your life in eternal things: God, His Word, and men's souls

What are we to learn from this parable?

1. This parable addresses the QUALITY of our work

2. When the judgment comes, our works will be tested by fire to see which ones survive

3. Works categorized as "gold, silver, costly stones" will survive and be rewarded; those characterized as "wood, hay or straw" will be burned up and not rewarded although their builders will still be saved

4. The critical information to understand here is what constitutes "gold, silver, costly stones." The answer is the three things that have eternal significance; God, God's Word and men's souls

5. Bear in mind that the other CROWN parables still apply. For example, if you are teaching a Sunday school class (men's souls), but you are doing it for the wrong reason, it will burn

The Various Crowns

The Scriptures are clear that there will be a Day of Judgment wherein a CROWN of righteousness will be awarded to those who have met God's criteria.

"From now on there is reserved for me the crown of righteousness, which the Lord, the righteous judge, will give me on that day, and not only to me but also to all who have longed for his appearing." 2 Timothy 4:8

All Christians will appear before the Judgment Seat of Christ, so that each of us may receive what is due us for the things done while in the body, whether good or bad.

"For all of us must appear before the judgment seat of Christ, so that each may receive recompense for what has been done in the body, whether good or evil." 2 Corinthians 5:10

The Bible talks about five different crowns that will be given to some of God's people when they enter into heaven. These crowns are going to be for work that is done for God that is beyond the normal scope of what the average Christian attempts to do.

They are like the trophies that are given to sports heroes or winning teams in sports; the difference is they are incorruptible and will last for eternity.

Think of a professional athlete and all that they go through to get ready for the season. They not only have to train but they have to watch their diets and weight to be able to compete in the sport they are in successfully. They give up a lot of their social life to stay in good shape. In other words, they do not live normal lives like the rest of us do.

Paul talks about people who run in these types of races and are forced to be temperate in the way they live their lives. They do it to obtain a perishable crown. Then Paul tells us that we should all run the race of this life to receive what will be an incorruptible or imperishable crown that can only be given by God the Father in heaven.

These very special crowns will be for Christians who went that extra mile and gave that extra individual effort in whatever God called them to do. There will be a distinctive mark or token given by our Lord to honor and reward any Christian who faithfully served Him in this life. The five crowns mentioned in the Bible are:

1. **The Crown of Righteousness:** This crown will go to those who have lived a good and righteous life for God.

2. **The Incorruptible Crown:** Bible scholars feel this is what some consider a "victor's crown." This crown is

called incorruptible. The New King James Version calls it an "imperishable" crown – the original King James Version calls it an "incorruptible" crown. Either way, it will be a crown that will last for all of eternity.

3. **The Crown of Life:** This next crown has been called by many the "martyr's crown." Jesus will give this crown to those who undergo severe hardship, testing, tribulation, and/or physical death on His behalf. Anyone willing to die for his or her faith in Jesus has given the ultimate sacrifice! It is the greatest act of bravery and courage that anyone can show God the Father.

4. **The Crown of Rejoicing:** This next crown has been called the "soul winner's crown." The Apostle Paul is calling those he has saved his "joy" and his "crown of rejoicing."

5. **The Crown of Glory:** This crown is for those who "shepherd" the flock of God. Shepherds lead the congregation into the ways and knowledge of God. They are teachers. These could be the Sunday school teachers, the pastors, and ministers who teach the Word of God in their ministries, or people who are appointed by God into the office of a teacher.

I believe God will be giving His teachers and shepherds this crown due to the extreme importance of bringing up others into the knowledge and ways of God.

Once you get saved, this is just the beginning. God wants you to grow in His knowledge and grace by reading the Bible and learning as much as you can about Him, His Son, and His Holy Spirit.

This is why teachers and shepherds are needed.

Most newborn Christians cannot understand the Bible the first time or two they read it. They need immediate help after they are saved to learn more about God and all of His ways.

This Chapter identifies five (5) criteria that will be rewarded by Christ on that day. I am not saying that these are all the criteria provided by Scripture, but these are explicitly promised. I have named each by using my favorite tool for remembering information – the acrostic. C-R-O-W-N.

As we go on through life, we realize that all of us were given different abilities, different attractiveness, different IQ's, different athletic strengths, musical talents, and on and on. For those of us who have accepted Christ as their Lord and Savior, we have been given the Holy Spirit who dispenses His GIFTS of the Spirit, and who nudges or brings to remembrance any applicable FRUIT of the Spirit in which we might need to grow. With these come the responsibility to apply them meaningfully to our lives. With these come the responsibility to apply them meaningfully to our lives.

Conclusion

All of these crowns will be permanent, incorruptible, and will never fade away. They will be eternal rewards bestowed upon those deemed to be deserving of them by God the Father for extraordinary service rendered on His behalf while living down here on this earth.

CHAPTER 7
How to Make Disciples

The Great Commission

"Now the eleven disciples went to Galilee, to the mountain to which Jesus had directed them. And when they saw him, they worshiped him, but some doubted. And Jesus came and said to them, 'All authority in heaven and on earth has been given to me. Go therefore and make disciples of all nations, baptizing them in the name of the Father and of the Son and of the Holy Spirit, teaching them to observe all that I have commanded you. And behold, I am with you always, to the end of the age.'" Matthew 28:16-20

In the first chapter of this book, I focused on the topic of the "The Three Greatest C's," the third of which was the Great Commission to make disciples. I have called the process of making disciples mentoring. It could also be called educating, teaching, coaching, one-on-one, etc. Of course, there are many definitions for these terms, but I define mentoring this way. Mentoring is a developmental process whereby one Christian helps another Christian climb higher in their MATURITY in the faith. Hence, mentoring is the process of making disciples and vice versa. It can occur with a brief encounter, but those relationships that have lasted a year or more are those that are more likely to affect lives profoundly. Mentoring happens in every field, but my use in this study is limited to Christian growth.

I have been a mentor for the 57 years of my Christian life. The primary venues were leading couples Bible studies, teaching Sunday School, marital and pre-marital counseling, and one-on-one mentoring. I received a Master's Degree in Counseling over twenty-five years ago. My predominant mentees have been college students from my forty plus years teaching on college campuses. This chapter comes from those years.

The logo above is for an organization called the Officers' Christian Fellowship (OCF). I have been affiliated with them since my conversion in 1961. Upon retirement from the US Army in 1979, I was asked to establish a ministry to officers and cadets at the United States Military Academy at West Point,

New York. I served in that role for eleven years. We met with the cadets one night a week, but my major responsibility five or six hours per day was mentoring them one on one in my office. I also formed a team of ten officer couples to help me with the ministry, two couples for each of the four regiments and two for administrative help. A major need expressed by college students was help in dating relationships. Chapter 5 is a product of that ministry,

You may be thinking that you alone have the responsibility to carry out the Great Commission. In fact, you should realize that the Holy Spirit has the greater responsibility. As presented in Chapter 2, the Holy Spirit assigns one or more of the Gifts of the Spirit to the new believer at the instant of his/her salvation. Each of these Gifts comes with abilities and as the four categories indicate – **SPECIAL** Gifts to **EQUIP** God's people, **SPEAKING** Gifts to **EXPLAIN** God's truth, **SERVING** Gifts to **ENABLE** God's work and **SIGN** Gifts to **ESTABLISH** God's authority. Think about it; those are gigantic ministries and responsibilities. Further, the Holy Spirit is always with you and will never forsake you 24/7. Also, consider the effect of the Fruit of the Spirit in helping us to **LOVE ONE ANOTHER.** Having spent my whole Christian life, over 57 years, making disciples, I unequivocally pronounce not to us, 'Oh Lord, not to us, but to Thy name be the glory.'

Qualities of a Mentor

- Foremost, the mentor's life must demonstrate Christian maturity beyond that of the mentee. He/she must walk their talk. "Your walk talks, and your talk talks, but if your walk does not talk louder than your talk talks, nobody pays any attention."

- "People do not care how much you know until they know how much you care." (Theodore Roosevelt)

- The mentor must be available, and their focus must be on the mentee's needs, not their own.

- The mentee must be accountable.

- The content of the relationship must be private and confidential. The mentor must act as a confidante and role model.

- The most significant predictor of positive outcomes is a close and trusting relationship.

- The mentor need not be an entirely mature Christian, just more mature than the mentee.

Mentoring relationships usually begin with the need for help with a specific problem. If the need is met and it exceeds expectations, this can often result in a mentoring relationship. The length of the relationship varies on the closeness and trust of the relationship. I have one (marriage counseling) that has lasted over twenty-seven years! I have another mentee (life skills) that has gone on for more than 14 years.

I must mention that certain precautions need to be observed in setting up a mentoring relationship. Foremost among these is sexuality. Some rules that I have adopted over the years follow:

- According to the Journal of American Law and Economics Review in 2000 the 60 to 80 percent of the divorces in the US are filed by women, not men. I meet with a woman one time to see if I could be of help. After that, the husband needs to attend also, and this has not been a problem.

- A situation must not only be right; it must look right.

- Because of the depth of personal situations that arise in mentoring, men should mentor men and women should mentor women. This is not a problem where there is a significant difference in their ages.

Make sure you set goals which help to keep the mentoring relationship focused. Without goals, a mentoring relationship can easily drift over to Christian fellowship. Goals should be SMART – Specific, Measurable, Action-oriented, Realistic (challenging, but achievable) and Timely. Of course, the first goal is solving the mentee's problem that led to the relationship.

It is essential that the mentee should be working with just one mentor at a time. The mentee can share whatever he/she desires to with whomever regarding what has taken place in the relationship. The mentor can share nothing without the mentee's permission.

There is a significant problem today in Christian ministries of not including the ministry of making disciples. The problem is that the scripturally prescribed method for bearing fruit, to include making disciples, is not being seriously followed. The second greatest "C" again is from Matthew 22:37: *"You shall love the Lord your God with all your heart and with all your soul and with all your mind."*

All means all! Now let's consider the key passage on bearing fruit from John 15:5,10, 15 – first the Scripture and then in diagram format:

John 15:5 *"I am the vine, you are the branches. Those who abide in me and I in them bear much fruit, because apart from me you can do nothing."* (ESV)

John 15:10 *"If you keep my commandments, you will abide in my love, just as I have kept my Father's commandments and abide in his love."*

John 15:15 *"I do not call you servants any longer, because the servant[b] does not know what the master is doing; but I have called you friends, because I have made known to you everything that I have heard from my Father."* (ESV)

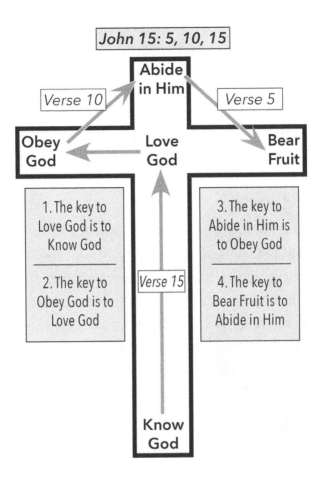

Bearing fruit does not merely mean volunteering to teach a Sunday School class or being an usher or a deacon. Bearing fruit biblically is not just "working for the Lord" or "doing Christian service," but the ministry that results from Knowing, Loving, Obeying, Abiding in God and Bearing Fruit. (KLOAB). The major problem is that it is too often not God working through our ministries to bear fruit, but us seeking to bear fruit via our energies. I confess that this has been a perennial problem for me through the years. I rush through my daily quiet times so I can get on with my plans for the day. "Beware of the barrenness of a busy life" describes this syndrome.

Busyness is just one of the problems that keep us away from abiding with God. Some other causes include pride, rebellion, self-centeredness, rationalization, audacity and the list goes on with reasons why I choose my way rather than God's way. Having now covered how not to bear fruit for God, let's follow the scriptural mandate of John 15.

Bearing fruit begins and ends with God's will. We must seek His will before moving on. Regretfully, this is not always immediately available, and we must wait for it. He reveals His will through a loving relationship with Him. It's important here for us to be seeking His will, not for us to be asking Him to bless our intention. Once we learn God's will, we must be obedient to it in love. Jesus measures our love by our obedience to His will, not by warm feelings.

"He who has my commandments and keeps them, he it is who loves me. And he who loves me will be loved by my Father, and I will love him and manifest myself to him." John 14:21

Thus far, I have introduced the key passage and its diagram which describe successful disciple-making. Now, let's skin dive deep into the verse to understand WHY it works and WHY it so frequently doesn't work.

In 1973, J.I. Packer wrote a book entitled, *Knowing God* which has now become a classic. My reason for mentioning this great book is to point out that the topic of knowing God is not even complete in a whole book, and positively, not in a few paragraphs.

When we know God and His will on a particular matter, and we are obedient to follow it, we are then abiding in Him, the closest state of all relationships. In this state, He now bears fruit through us! Knows, Loves, Obeys, Abides – Bears fruit!

In the next chapter, we'll see how Nehemiah models this correctly as he provides "An Anatomy of a Good Work." His relationship with God perfectly matches the requirements set out by Jesus. He abided with God 24/7.

CHAPTER 8
An Anatomy of a Good Work

The Great Commission

"Now the eleven disciples went to Galilee, to the mountain to which Jesus had directed them. And when they saw him they worshiped him, but some doubted. And Jesus came and said to them, 'All authority in heaven and on earth has been given to me. Go therefore and make disciples of all nations, baptizing them in the name of the Father and of the Son and of the Holy Spirit, teaching them to observe all that I have commanded you. And behold, I am with you always, to the end of the age.'" Matthew 28:16-20 (ESV)

The Scriptures are clear that a Christian's day-to-day life is to manifest growth in the production of good fruit by Abiding in Christ. – John 15:5 (ESV)

"I am the vine; you are the branches. Whoever abides in me and I in him, he it is that bears much fruit, for apart from me you can do nothing."

This chapter identifies six (6) criteria that together make up an anatomy of a good work. I have named each requirement via letters of an acrostic – SPENCER. These criteria were derived from a study of the Book of Nehemiah, from which I use tbe letter "N" in the middle of the word SPENCER.

There may be some of the readers of this book who have never heard of the man Nehemiah. The time frame for this story is approximately 445 B.C. – 432 B.C. At that time Jerusalem was governed by the Persian King Cyrus. It was his 20th year and Nehemiah was his cupbearer. Cyrus issued a decree ultimately permitting about 50,000 captives to return to Jerusalem including Nehemiah who was to oversee the rebuilding of the city walls. The story, though is the backdrop because I believe Nehemiah abided with God more than any other person in all of Scripture, excluding Christ. Many challenges needed to be faced and dealt with and in each one Nehemiah turned first to God, the One he wanted to hear and obey. His joy was complete as God answered his prayers one by one for God's goal and glory. The following Scripture provides a more detailed description of Nehemiah's execution of the "pray and plan" principle. May his life and walk with the Lord motivate you as it has me.

"Now it happened in the month of Chislev, in the twentieth year, as I was in Susa the citadel, that Hanani, one of my brothers, came with certain men from Judah. And I asked them concerning the Jews who escaped, who had survived the exile, and concerning Jerusalem. And they said to me, 'The remnant there in the province who had survived the exile is in great trouble and shame. The wall of Jerusalem is broken down, and its gates are destroyed by fire.'" Nehemiah 1:1-3 (ESV)

For us living in a police-protected society today, we can only imagine their situation. The walls being broken down meant that any nearby king could attack and take whatever he wanted. The gates were broken down and could not be locked at night. This made it possible for gangs to invade, kill and capture any and all in Jerusalem.

1. "S" Be Sensitive and Get Involved

From these verses, we learn that Nehemiah was in Susa the capital when his brother Hanani returned from a visit to Jerusalem. Hanani shared that Jerusalem's walls had been broken down, its gates destroyed by fire, and that the remaining Jews there were in great trouble and shame. These Jews were considered invaders, so revenge was very likely. Nehemiah's reaction to this report is spelled out in Nehemiah 1:4: *"As soon as I heard these words I sat down and wept and mourned for days, and I continued fasting and praying before the God of heaven."* We learn from subsequent verses that this praying and fasting went on for at least four months before he mentioned it to his boss, the king!

"S" Be Sensitive and Get Involved

SITUATION	NEHEMIAH'S RESPONSE	RESULT	PRINCIPLE
Walls & Gates Destoyed	Great Sensitivity, Weeping, Fasting	Turned to God in soul prayer	Prayer first ALWAYS

What are we to learn from this passage?

1. Once again, there may be something more you can do after you have prayed, but there is nothing more you can do until you have prayed!

2. Nehemiah's great love for God caused him to be sensitive to the Jews' situation.

3. Nehemiah's first action always was to seek God through prayer and fasting.

4. You won't get involved unless God's needs are more important than your needs.

5. Nehemiah justified his request for help from the king based on his performance to the king, *"if I have found favor...."*

2. "P" Pray and Plan

Immediate – and persistent.

We learn from verse 4 that Nehemiah's first response to the news was that he began praying and fasting. This beautifully portrayed the nature of Nehemiah's prayer life: intimate; personal verses show its depth and maturity – abiding!

Nehemiah 1:5-11 (ESV): *"And I said, 'O LORD God of heaven, the great and awesome God (ADORATION) who keeps covenant and steadfast love with those who love him and keep his commandments, let your ear be attentive and your eyes open, to hear the prayer of your* (SUPPLICATION) *servant that I now pray before you day and night for the people of Israel your servants, confessing the sins of the people of Israel, which we have sinned against you. Even I and my father's house have sinned.* (CONFESSION) *We have acted very corruptly against you and have not kept the commandments, the statutes, and the rules that you commanded your servant Moses. Remember the word that you commanded your servant Moses, saying, 'If you are unfaithful, I will scatter you among the peoples, but if you return to me and keep my commandments and do them, though your outcasts are in the uttermost parts of heaven, from there I will gather them and bring them to the place that I have chosen, to make my name dwell there.' They are your servants and your people, whom you have redeemed by your great power and by your strong hand.* (THANKSGIVING) *O Lord, let your ear be at attentive to the prayer of your servant, and to the prayer of your servants who delight to fear your name, and give success to your servant today,* (SUPPLICATION) *and grant him mercy in the sight of this man.*

Now I was cupbearer to the king."

As verse 11 brings to a close these four months, we see that Nehemiah announces that he was the cupbearer to the king and that he believes the time is right for him to make the request the Lord has laid on his heart.

"P" Pray and Plan

SITUATION	NEHEMIAH'S RESPONSE	RESULT	PRINCIPLE
Nehemiah before the King and Queen as cupbearer	Responded to the King with God's Plan	King fully approved the Plan	Good works begin with sensitivity to others' needs

What are we to learn from this Bible story?

1. God creates life situations that test our faith

2. God is always there when called upon

3. Those receiving God's blessings come to God as sinners, not as saints deserving to be recognized and rewarded (CONFESSION)

3. "E" Elicit Timely and Total Support - Make Physical Preparation

SPENCER is an effective acrostic for citing the six elements of a good work, but as I have been pointing out, these elements often occur randomly like "expect opposition and obstacles" may occur at any point in the sequence, etc. So, in the case of Nehemiah, opposition began to show itself in Chapter 2. This is why we read of Nehemiah's asking the king to write a letter authorizing the rebuilding of the walls. In addition to having the king's support from Susa, and following their arrival in Jerusalem, he called the Jewish leaders together for their consensus and support as well.

"E" Elicit Timely and Total Support - Make Physical Preparation

SITUATION	NEHEMIAH'S RESPONSE	RESULT	PRINCIPLE
Nehemiah needed King's support as well as the local Jewish leaders	Nehemiah called together sources of Jewish power	Nehemiah got all the local support that he needed	Pray first then organization are the winning combination

What are we to learn from this Bible story?

1. Many needs in life are never met because no one was sensitive to the need and/or no one planned how to fix them

2. God is called upon too infrequently to meet needs

3. When duties are assigned, there must be accountability

4. Nehemiah was successful because although he was present during construction, he was praying and was participating in the construction as well.

The **N** in - S P E **"N"** C E R - **Stands For Nehemiah**

4. "C" Continue Praying and Be Vigilant

Thus far we have heard about this whole story from Nehemiah's perspective. The following is an account of both the locals and Nehemiah's responces. Only in Chapter 2 verse 19 (ESV) do we have any idea of what the non-Jewish locals thought about this.

Developing situation: *"But when Sanballat the Horonite and Tobiah the Ammonite servant and Geshem the Arab heard of it, they jeered at us and despised us and said, 'What is this thing that you are doing? Are you rebelling against the king?'"* The principle teaching is God's at work in our fallen world, and His work is initiated through the FAITH and PRAYER of His people. We learn this from Chapter 4 (ESV) as follows:

"Now when Sanballat heard that we were building the wall, he was angry and greatly enraged, and he jeered at the Jews. And he said in the presence of his brothers and of the army of Samaria, 'What are these feeble Jews doing? Will they restore it for themselves? Will they sacrifice? Will they finish up in a day? Will they revive the stones out of the heaps of rubbish, and burned ones at that?' Tobiah the Ammonite was beside him, and he said, 'Yes, what they are building—if a fox goes up on it he will break down their stone wall!' Hear, O our God, (SUPPLICATION) for we are despised. Turn back their taunt on their own heads and give them up to be plundered in a land where they are captives. Do not cover their guilt, and let not their sin be blotted out from your sight, for they have provoked you to anger in the presence of the builders."

I am constrained at this point to emphasize a significant point. First, it's not SPENCER! It was that Nehemiah was abiding with God. The principle teaching is God's at work in our fallen world. And that work is PRAYER and FAITH — abiding! Nehemiah's every waking moment was lived out in prayer and faith. He indeed walked with God, and hopefully, that will be your response. Nehemiah 4:9 captures this principle: *"And we prayed to our God and set a guard as a protection against them day and night."* (ESV)

SITUATION	NEHEMIAH'S RESPONSE	RESULT	PRINCIPLE
The locals began to organize against the Jews	Prayed to God and increased security day & night	The wall continued to be built ahead of schedule!	This was God's working through Faith & Prayer

"C" Continue Praying and Be Vigilant

5. "E" Expect Opposition and Obstacles

As noted above, we must always expect that there will be opposition and obstacles to the changes we are proposing. Most of us do not like change; we like the status quo. When groups encounter pressure to change, as was the case here of the non-Jews in Jerusalem, or when isolated individuals or groups form to resist change, their methodology is predictable as we see from the following four states: rational argument, emotional seduction, attack and amputation.

Nehemiah 4:6-20: *"So we built the wall. And all the wall was joined together to half its height, for the people had a mind to work.*

"But when Sanballat and Tobiah and the Arabs and the Ammonites and the Ashdodites heard that the repairing of the walls of Jerusalem was going forward and that the breaches were beginning to be closed, they were very angry. And they all plotted together to come and fight against Jerusalem and to cause confusion in it. And we prayed to our God and set a guard as a protection against them day and night. (SUPPLICATION)

"In Judah it was said, "The strength of those who bear the burdens is failing. There is too much rubble. By ourselves we will not be able to rebuild the wall." And our enemies said, "They will not know or see till we come among them and kill them and stop the work." At that time the Jews who lived near them came from all directions and said to us ten times, "You must return to us." So in the lowest parts of the space behind the wall, in open places, I stationed the people by their clans, with their swords, their spears, and their bows. And I looked and arose and said to the nobles and to the officials and to the rest of the people, "Do not be afraid of them. Remember the Lord, (ADORATION) who is great and awesome, and fight for your brothers, your sons, your daughters, your wives, and your homes."

"When our enemies heard that it was known to us and that God had frustrated their plan, we all returned to the wall, each to his work. From that day on, half of

my servants worked on construction, and half held the spears, shields, bows, and coats of mail. And the leaders stood behind the whole house of Judah, who were building on the wall. Those who carried burdens were loaded in such a way that each labored on the work with one hand and held his weapon with the other. And each of the builders had his sword strapped at his side while he built. The man who sounded the trumpet was beside me. And I said to the nobles and to the officials and to the rest of the people, "The work is great and widely spread, and we are separated on the wall, far from one another. In the place where you hear the sound of the trumpet, rally to us there. Our God will fight for us." (ESV)

"E" Expect Opposition and Obstacles

SITUATION	NEHEMIAH'S RESPONSE	RESULT	PRINCIPLE
The threat of war intensified as the walls were filled in	Nehemiah knew there would be a war and he organized for it	The Jews fully complied with Nehemiah's leadership	The unity of the Jewish community under God was powerful

What are we to learn from these passages?

1. What had gone so well with the king and his subjects caused the locals to begin to unite against the Jews.

2. The threat of war followed its predicted formula: Rational argument, emotional seduction, attack, amputation.

3. Nehemiah never doubted God's love for the Jews nor His commitment to their eventual victory.

4. Nehemiah's counterattack plan (God) gave the Jew's success.

6. "R" Resist Diversions and Persevere

The war with the locals was not the only challenge faced by Nehemiah. Nehemiah Chapter 5 begins with the words *"Now there arose a great outcry of the people and of their wives against their Jewish brothers. For there were those who said, 'With our sons and our daughters, we are many. So let us get grain, that we may eat and keep alive.' There were also those who said, 'We are mortgaging our fields, our vineyards, and our houses to get grain because of the famine.'"* (ESV)

Another diversion to rebuilding the walls was internal. Although taxes had to be paid to the king, the nobles and officials were taking an undue amount of interest to line their pockets, necessitating the Jewish brothers having to sell their fields, vineyards, orchards, houses, and even family members. This made Nehemiah *"very angry!"* He then called all the nobles and officials together and told them their behaviors had to change. They were speechless. This diversion ended with the words: *"And all the assembly said 'Amen' and praised the LORD. And the people did as they had promised."* (the joy of abiding!) Also at this time, Nehemiah was appointed the governor in the land of Judah.

Going forward we learn in the following passages more about Nehemiah's character; namely his heart of compassion for his people, for justice, righteousness, his generosity and willingness to hold those guilty to God's standard on behalf of the Jewish brothers being taken advantage of.

Nehemiah 5:6-19 (ESV): *"I was very angry when I heard their outcry and these words. I took counsel with myself, and I brought charges against the nobles and the officials. I said to them, "You are exacting interest, each from his brother." And I held a great assembly against them and said to them, "We, as far as we are able, have bought back our Jewish brothers who have been sold to the nations, but you even sell your brothers that they may be sold to us!" They were silent and could not find a word to say. So I said, "The thing that you are doing is not good. Ought you not to walk in the fear of our God to prevent the taunts of the nations our enemies? Moreover, I and my brothers and my servants are lending them money and grain. Let us abandon this exacting of interest. Return to them this very day their fields, their vineyards, their olive orchards, and their houses, and the percentage of money, grain, wine, and oil that you have been exacting from them." Then they said, "We will restore these and require nothing from them. We will do as you say." And I called the priests and made them swear to do as they had promised. I also shook out the fold of my garment and said, "So may God shake out every man from his house and from his labor who does not keep this promise. So may he be shaken out and emptied." And all the assembly said "Amen" and praised the LORD. And the people did as they had promised.* (Abide, abide, abide!)

"Moreover, from the time that I was appointed to be their governor in the land of Judah, from the twentieth year to the thirty-second year of Artaxerxes the king, twelve years, neither I nor my brothers ate the food allowance of the governor. The former governors who were before me laid heavy burdens on the people and took from them for their daily ration forty shekels of silver. Even their servants lorded it over the people. (Nehemiah's example) But I did not do so, because of the fear of God. I also persevered in the work on this wall, and we acquired no land, and all my servants were gathered there for the work. Moreover, there were at my table 150 men, Jews and officials, besides those who came to us from the nations that were around us. Now what was prepared at my expense for each day was one ox and six choice sheep and birds, and every ten days all kinds of wine in abundance. Yet for all this I did not demand the food allowance of the governor, because the service was too heavy on this people. Remember for my good, O my God, all that I have done for this people."

In a book called *Good to Great* written by Jim Collins he notes that the prominent companies in America were all led by what he termed Level 5 Leaders. These leaders were not only great because of their skills in managing their companies, but he found them to have a second characteristic – HUMILITY. Chapter 5 and 6 of Nehemiah render him as not just a good leader, but a great leader!

Nehemiah Chapter 6 introduces a final diversion that Nehemiah had to deal with, a conspiracy against him. Nehemiah's enemies continued to try to kill Nehemiah and stop the work. In Nehemiah 6:1-9 (ESV) we read:

"Now when Sanballat and Tobiah and Geshem the Arab and the rest of our enemies heard that I had built the wall and that there was no breach left in it (although up to that time I had not set up the doors in the gates), Sanballat and Geshem sent to me, saying, "Come and let us meet together at Hakkephirim in the plain of Ono." But they intended to do me harm. And I sent messengers to them, saying, "I am doing a great work and I cannot come down. Why should the work stop while I leave it and come down to you?" And they sent to me four times in this way, and I answered them in the same manner. In the same way Sanballat for the fifth time sent his servant to me with an open letter in his hand. In it was written, "It is reported among the nations, and Geshem also says it, that you and the Jews intend to rebel; that is why you are building the wall. And according to these reports you wish to become their king. And you have also set up prophets to proclaim concerning you in Jerusalem, 'There is a king in Judah.' And now the king will hear of these reports. So now come and let us take counsel together." Then I sent to him, saying, "No such things as you say have been done, for you are inventing them out of your own mind." For they all wanted to frighten us, thinking, "Their hands will drop from the work, and it will not be done." But now, O God, strengthen my hands.

"R" Resist Diversions and Persevere

SITUATION	NEHEMIAH'S RESPONSE	RESULT	PRINCIPLE
Diversions are a normal part of any job. We must recognize and deal with them	Some must be dealt with as those Nehemiah dealt with	Today cell phones and social media present new diversions which must be dealt with	Keep the main thing in mind and avoid diversions

Why did I choose to use Nehemiah as a biblical example of a Level 5 leader? Because more than any other person in the Scriptures, except Christ, he appears to personify the six principles present in the *Anatomy of a Good Work* – SPENCER. At the core of his life, he desires to obey God, and walk with God with all his heart, mind, soul and body. He never asked God to bless Nehemiah's plan because Nehemiah's plans were always God's plans, constantly updated and abided within a moment-by-moment relationship with the One to whom he owed his ultimate allegiance.

What have you learned from this study of Nehemiah?

1. Truly, Nehemiah provides an outstanding Anatomy of a Good Work.

2. Truly, there are no examples of greater faith in God than Nehemiah.

3. Truly, Nehemiah models turning to God before any other resource — ACTS.

4. Truly Nehemiah provides an outstanding leadership model — SPENCER

EPILOGUE

Since being faced with the news of impending death and hospice care my thoughts turned to my response to this situation. I have chosen the higher road, deciding to write a book to encourage and challenge its readers to a higher calling – living the Christian life versus operating as Christians using the world's principles.

In bottom line terms, I believe that most Christians, myself included, have unknowingly lived our Christian lives operating under the misunderstanding of God's will. Specifically, we Christians seem to be under the same pressure living the Christian life from the world's perspective. Chapter 6 (CROWN) would enforce such a mindset, that success in the Christian life is just like that of the world except we have a different boss. Quotations like "Beware of the barrenness of a busy life" are all too evidenced.

What lifestyle produces the most joyous life for the person and for the Lord? I believe that I discovered what it is. Many will be shocked to learn this key to the Christian life. The key is prayer!

John 15:11 – *"I have said these things to you so that my joy may be in you, and that your joy may be complete."*

It turns out that the most important activity of our Christian life is prayer. And, as presented in the book, it is not the quiet time we may have every morning, nor is it attending church regularly, nor all other Christian activities of our lives such as teaching Sunday School class or leading a Bible study.

It is prayer with our God 24/7 or as I have described in today's language – it is "hanging out" with God all day every day! Wherever we go, He goes with us – to take a shower, to drive to work, to mow the lawn. God named this activity as "abiding" with Him as presented in John 15:5, 10, 15. From these passages we learn that the prerequisites of abiding are **knowing** Him, **loving** Him and **obeying** Him with the key being obeying. This 24/7 obedience then governs what we do each day, where we go, how we treat others, etc. And with all of these come the most joyous lives on earth. And now we come full circle to where we began in Chapter 1, the first Greatest "C," *"Come to me, all you who are weary and burdened, and I will give you rest." Take my yoke upon you and learn from me, for I am gentle and humble in heart, and you will find rest for your souls. For my yoke is easy and my burden is light."* Matthew 11:28-30 (NIV)